THE MAJOR WORKS
of
R.N. ELLIOTT

THE MAJOR WORKS
of
R.N. ELLIOTT

Edited, foreworded, and with a biography
by Robert R. Prechter, Jr.

Published by NEW CLASSICS LIBRARY, INC.

THE MAJOR WORKS OF R.N. ELLIOTT

Printed in the United States of America
by Haddon Craftsmen, Inc., New York City

First Printing: March 1980
Second Printing: April 1984
Third Printing: March 1987
Second Edition (with expanded biography): December 1990

For information, address the publishers:
New Classics Library, Inc.
P.O. Box 1618
Gainesville, Georgia 30503
USA

ISBN: 0-932750-15-X
Library of Congress Catalog Card Number: 80-80273

The illustration on p. 232 is from The Secret Teachings of All Ages by Manly P. Hall and is reprinted by permission of The Philosophical Research Society.

This book is dedicated to A. John Frost, who has developed more innovative thought with regard to the philosophy of the Wave Principle than any man since R. N. Elliott himself.

ACKNOWLEDGEMENTS

A number of people have been instrumental in this project. A. J. Frost provided a copy of <u>The Wave Principle</u>, copies of the Elliott Wave Supplements to the Bank Credit Analyst, and collaborated on the forewording comments. The New York Public Library yielded much information, and is the only library known to have a copy of Nature's Law. Charles J. Collins, Peter Kendall, Howard Fay and Brenda Taylor were also helpful in providing biographical information. Marie Eliades took the photo of R.N. Elliott's house in L.A. Paul Brodtkorb took the photo of R.N. Elliott's apartment house in Brooklyn. Claire Chartrand, an associate of the late Hamilton Bolton, helped clear up a few cloudy areas on the available reproductions. Alfred H. Kingon, editor-in-chief of <u>Financial World</u> magazine, generously consented to the republication of Elliott's 1939 articles. Arthur Merrill of Merrill Analysis, Inc. provided his invaluable photographic talents toward the production of the camera-ready manuscript.

One of the main reasons a comprehensive republication of Elliott's works has not been attempted before was the prospect of the formidable illustrating job necessary to do justice to Elliott's concepts. His two books are rather roughly illustrated and a mere photographic reproduction would not have sufficed. Robin Machcinski successfully tackled this job and we're proud to feature her work herein.

The jacket design was crafted by graphics artist Irene Prechter of New Orleans, Louisiana.

CONTENTS

149 NATURE'S LAW -- THE SECRET OF THE UNIVERSE
(1946)

NOTE: Mr. Prechter is a collector of Elliott memorabilia and would appreciate knowing of any such material available. He would also welcome any additional knowledge concerning R. N. Elliott, no matter how trivial, which has gone unnoticed.

Hamilton Bolton said in 1953, "For every one hundred investors who have heard of the Dow Theory, there is probably not one who knows about Elliott's Wave Principle." In the service of justice, the time has come to remedy this oversight of history.

For decades a demand has existed for reprints of Elliott's major works, but until now no one has seen fit to bring all the books and articles together in one professionally illustrated volume. THE MAJOR WORKS has been published in response to demand from readers of Frost's and my book and out of my deep concern that the form of the original discovery not be lost in the dust bin of history. It is for those who have an appreciation for the historical record and who wish an understanding of the development of the Wave Principle through its discoverer, R.N. Elliott, that this book is published.

History is replete with examples of innovators and discoverers, men years or even centuries before their time, whose ideas reached so far ahead of their contemporaries' that they were ignored by the professional establishment of their day. While Elliott was not ignored, he most certainly was not afforded the recognition he deserved.

In my experience there are two categories of people who have stood in the way of providing Elliott's Wave Principle a wider audience. The first is made up of those who reject it, including both those who dismiss any such ideas out of hand, and those who grasp the theory but choose not to believe it because they will not expend the energy required to find out if it is true.

A neutral response to unreasonable rejection of the Wave Principle would undoubtedly have been impossible to the discoverer of this incredible phenomenon, who undoubtedly feared his discovery would go entirely unnoticed if he weren't able to convince at least a portion of the investment world of its validity. The intensity with which Nature's Law is written, for instance, partly derives from Elliott's desire to convince the investment establishment not only that the Wave Principle was a valid theory, but that it was the truth behind the progression of the stock market, and that in fact it reflected the law governing the form of the natural path of all human activities. My goal, however, is not necessarily to convince readers that "Elliott is the way," but merely to make available the knowledge of the Wave Principle to those who have enough sense and energy to use it.

As for the second category, I find that of those people who understand the theory's immense value and apply it successfully, most have done their best to keep it secret. I have been asked several times by students of the Wave Principle to refrain from publishing any material at all on Elliott's great innovative work for fear that "too many" people would start using the Wave Principle in their investment timing, thus diluting the utility of the theory.

I must say that at times I have had second thoughts. The Wave Principle frequently can call turns and project targets with such incredible accuracy that I still find myself amazed. And as a tool for explaining the otherwise surprising and indecipherable ways of the market, it has no equal.

However, the reader must realize that, despite the basic simplicity of the concept itself, "Elliott" analysis is not that easy to do if your goal is to do it well. On the other hand, it is very easy to do haphazardly, and most part time practicioners do exactly that. Even if the Wave Principle were to become popular, there would be so many opportunistic hacks floating about their ill considered opinions that the truth probably would be lost to the investment majority in the ensuing babble.

In addition, let me say that it is one easy thing to recognize that the Wave Principle governs stock prices while it is quite another to predict the next wave, and still another to profit from the exercise, as anyone who ever has attempted to turn any good market forecasting approach into money knows full well. None of us can escape our humanness, a humanness which works as part of the universal design whether we wish it to or not. I have yet to meet a man who invested or traded with a

completely rational program based on reasonable probabilities without allowing his greed, his fear, his
extraneous opinions or his irrelevant judgments to
interfere. To such a superman of discipline, the Wave
Principle would yield a fortune; but then so would many
other methods. What no other method of reading the
market can give you, however, which the Elliott Wave
Principle makes possible for the first time, is a
framework within which to observe, reflect upon and
enjoy the beauty of nature in the social activity of man.

Thus, in the end, I find myself persuaded by the
words of both Elliott and Collins, who agreed in their
letters that what is important above all else is the "search
for Truth." This search is a project for all mankind, and
keeping dramatic new concepts from others will only
hinder progress. After all, the Wave Principle indeed
may be Nature's way of giving us a peek at the future.

We must realize, of course, that it is only a
peek, not the full panorama. Foretelling the future with
exactitude all the time is not one of the blessings
available to man, and likely never will be. Elliott himself,
despite his great achievement, was not fanatical about his
ideas. He knew that the Wave Principle, for all of its
value, was not the be-all and end-all. "The discovery of
the Wave Principle," he said, "has only opened the door to
real progress."

As you read Elliott's works, it may help to
recall his words of guidance to Charles J. Collins when he
said, "I hope you appreciate that application of rules
requires considerable practice and a tranquil mind."

—*Falcofoto*

R. N. Elliott

A BIOGRAPHY OF R.N. ELLIOTT

by

ROBERT R. PRECHTER, JR.

AUTHORS' NOTE

Until now, nothing whatsoever had appeared in print pertaining to Elliott's personal life or his activities prior to discovering the Wave Principle. The facts I was able to put together were gleaned partly by studying the books he wrote, corresponding with the Library of Congress and talking with former associates. Journalist Peter Kendall followed several leads to excellent result. My deepest gratitude, however, goes to Charles J. Collins, who sent me the entire file of early letters between Elliott and himself. Not only was that file one of the most exciting collections of material I have ever read, but the letters told more than any other source about the story of Elliott and his discovery of the most conceptually fascinating and useful description of market behavior in existence.

As you read the story of Mr. R. N. Elliott, you may be as intrigued as I am that a theory so remarkably unique, when compared to other methods of market analysis at that time and even those of today, could have been developed so late in life by a man not of Wall Street background. Bolton accurately described the enormity of Elliott's feat when he said that "he developed his principle into a rational method of stock market analysis <u>on a scale never before attempted</u>."

That Elliott was intellectually honest is unquestionable. That his theories evolved independently, with little input from previous researchers, is fascinating.

The Pre-Discovery Years

Ralph Nelson Elliott was born a U.S. citizen (probably in Los Angeles, California) in 1871. In his youth he was employed variously as a telegraph operator, stenographer, train dispatcher, station agent and lineman at the height of America's great railroad boom. Around 1896, he chose to enter the accounting profession* and quickly developed the specialty fields of railroad accounting and restaurant accounting. He spent the next six years of his life in New York City as a restaurant accountant and in the process became quite familiar with the Wall Street area, where he apparently prepared accounting reports for some restaurants in the financial district.

Although based in New York, Elliott traveled extensively, and for the following twenty-five years held executive positions primarily with railroad companies in Mexico and Central America, serving foremost in accounting and company reorganization. His career included travel to Canada, Germany, England and France. His largest reorganization outside the railroad field was Amsinck & Co., an export-import house of five hundred employees. At one point in his career he was selected by Dr. Jeremiah Henks, then Chairman of the Alexander Hamilton Institute in New York, to straighten out the fiscal affairs of Nicaragua. As a result of his long stay in Central America, he became as fluent in Spanish, both spoken and written, as in English.

During the early 1920s, Elliott began focusing again on his restaurant accounting specialty, contributing regular articles on the subject to <u>Tea Room and Gift Shop Magazine</u>. His renown grew to the extent that in 1924 Columbia University invited him to speak on the subject, an offer which he was forced to decline as he was once

---

* Ironically, some researchers may have concluded that Elliott was an accountant due to the fact that there are library records of a Mr. R. N. Elliott (F.C.A.) who did a study for the Institute of Chartered Accountants in Australia. Despite the superficial similarities, these records refer to different people.

again on his way out of New York on business. Shortly thereafter, he began writing a book about his field of experience. In 1926, while serving his last professional position as the Auditor General of the International Railways of Central America in Guatemala, he completed a small but comprehensive volume entitled Tea Room and Cafeteria Management, which was published in August of that year by Little, Brown & Co. The first favorable review appeared in the New York Herald Tribune (and apparently its international edition as well) on August 8. In November, Elliott returned to New York to help develop and execute promotion for the book, which sold for $1.50, from his temporary base at the Wolcott Hotel on Fifth Avenue. Elliott was overflowing with promotional ideas and enthusiasm, as numerous communications with the publisher attest. The book, a thorough, practical guide on opening and managing a restaurant, dealt primarily with "the economical aspects of the preparation of food as a business." Elliott's book paid meticulous attention to detail, not only concerning the financial end of the business, but the aesthetic as well. He gave great attention to detailing, arranging, analyzing, and planning, methods which are suggestive of some aspects of the Wave Principle and which may indicate why it was this particular man who was able to discover it. Several passages in the volume reveal bits and pieces of Elliott's background and personality, as well as his interests.

In his book on restaurant accounting, Elliott displayed a subtle sense of humor, a quality which was not evident in his later writings. For instance, after discussing the absolute necessity of obtaining adequate capital for start-up purposes, a precondition which many would-be restaurateurs he knew had naively insisted upon ignoring, he commented as follows:

> On the other hand, circumstances may arise where, there being a real demand for a restaurant in a certain neighborhood, patronage may be relied upon from the start. Such conditions, coupled with the possible fact that the owner possesses in that particular locality a house furnished with all necessary equipment which can be utilized for the purpose of a tea room, may be successfully taken advantage of to open a restaurant with very little initial outlay. Here the owner will pay no additional rent and will, so to

TEA ROOM AND CAFETERIA MANAGEMENT

By R. N. ELLIOTT

Mr. Elliott, for many years an organizer and analyst in various lines of business, has recently specialized in tea rooms and cafeterias. In this book he aims to prevent the inexperienced from losing their precious capital and to assist owners in making the greatest possible profit.

He has covered every aspect of the business, from the choice of a location to making out the income-tax report, touching on rentals, names, equipment, decoration, help and menus; on buying, on advertising, the system of accounting and other matters of vital importance which may be easily overlooked or improperly handled. This informative volume should certainly open the eyes of any one pot fully acquainted with the details of tea room and cafeteria management and will undoubtedly help many an owner to get far better returns on his investment.

Mr. Elliott is already known to many tea room and cafeteria managers through his regular contributions to the *Tea Room and Gift Shop Magazine*.

Contents: Capital: Location and Accommodations; Leases and Ventilation; Decorations; Names and Signs; Hostesses; Food and Menus; Portions; Pricing Food on Menus; Necessity for Accounting; Analysis of Expenses: Insurance; Repairs. Replacements and Taxes; Reconciliation of Bank Balances; Employees. Their Wages, Schedules; Tea Room and Cafeteria Compared; Fluctuations; Surplus Food or "Left-Overs"; Buying; A Quiet Kitchen; Advertising; Public Opinion of Your Tea Room; Lists of Equipment; Conclusion.

176 pages. 12mo. Cloth. $1.50

Boston   LITTLE, BROWN & COMPANY   Publishers

Tea Room and Cafeteria Management

by R. N. Elliott

Price $1.50

This new book offers an invaluable guide to owners and managers as well as to prospective entrants into the tea room and cafeteria business, every phase of which is here discussed.

speak, merely assume the responsibility of feeding a larger family. He may also, more nearly to invest himself with all the Utopian advantages, be possessed of a vegetable garden, chicken run and perhaps a cow or two.

Several paragraphs in Elliott's book reveal his interest in business cycles. Business cycles played a paramount role in Elliott's profession and his interest in them was obviously keen. In a chapter entitled "Fluctuations," he commented:

It is a well-known fact that prosperity and depression follow each other in cycles and the waves of these are extremely variable, but nevertheless certain. This is not the place to discuss cycles; suffice it to say that they are very real.

Elliott referred to business cycles in his conclusion poetically as "the ebb and flow of circumstance," a phrase which uses the liquid metaphor he later called "waves."

The future was of great concern to Elliott. In a chapter entitled "Necessity for Accounting," he explained:

Accounting, like everything else, is undergoing very radical steps in evolution. It is becoming serviceable in a vastly broader sense. Accounts, records and statistics ⌊are kept⌋ with a view to making a report that contains not only the essential data for the moment but primarily serves as a guide for future operations.

Perhaps the outlook expressed in that last sentence eventually led him to a study of forecasting the stock market.

After returning briefly to Guatemala, Elliott retired from his position with the Central American railways due to contracting a severe alimentary tract illness caused by the organism amoeba histolytica. He left Guatemala for an apartment hotel suite at 548 South Spring Street, Los Angeles in January 1927 in hope of recovering from the malady which had stricken him.

Despite suffering from the symptoms of his illness, Elliott spent the first half of 1927 aggressively marketing his book, getting copies into bookstores, arranging for reviews and obtaining lists for the mailing of circulars, ultimately to the end of securing clients for his newly independent professional business as an "Expert Restaurant Accountant." Additional favorable reviews poured in from The New York World, the National Restaurant Association, which invited him to speak in Buffalo, New York on September 26, and others. Ads for the book were placed in Good Housekeeping. In December 1927, after years of intense work, travel, and hotel living, Elliott secured a more permanent residence at 833 Beacon Avenue.

Instead of enjoying the recovery he required, however, Elliott's illness continued to worsen. By 1929

833 Beacon Avenue, Los Angeles. Elliott's home from 1927 to 1937(8).
Photo 1990 by Marie Eliades.

his condition had developed into a debilitating case of pernicious anemia, involving chronic fever, dysentery and weight loss, leaving him bedridden. Elliott's efforts at establishing a specialized consulting business had to be abandoned. Several times over the next five years Elliott came extremely close to death, but each time managed to recover.

After several trying years of extreme illness, Elliott's health improved, but not to full recovery. Although his physical energy was low, he still needed something to occupy his mind while spending long hours recuperating in a chair on the front porch. As circumstances would have it, Elliott was living then through the most exciting period in U.S. stock market history, the roaring bull market of the 1920s and, at the time of his worsening illness, the most dramatic bear market smash on record. He read Robert Rhea's book on Dow Theory and became one of the first subscribers to Rhea's stock market service, Dow Theory Comment (1932-1937). It was sometime during this period that Elliott turned his full attention to studying the behavior of the stock market.

The Discovery

For several years Elliott devoted himself to his new area of study. Not unlike Dow Theory genius Robert Rhea, who suffered from tuberculosis and was bedridden at the time, Elliott began to make some fascinating observations concerning the movement of prices on Wall Street. His observations of general stock market behavior were gleaned through a dedicated, almost obsessive research. He undertook a long and painstaking study of yearly, monthly, weekly, daily, hourly, and even half hourly charts of the various indexes covering seventy-five years of stock market behavior. He constructed the hourly charts from a data series which began for the Dow Jones Industrial Average in April 1933, and the half hourly charts from data he collected off the tape in the trading room of a brokerage house.

Elliott's theory of the Wave Principle was formulated entirely from empirical evidence. Around

May 1934, just two months after his final brush with
death, Elliott's observations of stock market behavior
began falling together into a general set of principles
which applied to all degrees of wave movement in the
stock price averages. When he started applying these
principles over the next several months to expectations
for the future path of the market, he felt, as he later put
it, "something like the inventor who is trying to become
proficient as an operator of a machine of his own design."
As he got more proficient in the application of his principles, they began to amaze him with their accuracy.

At this point in his life, Elliott's finances were
at a dangerous low. His savings, which had appeared more
than adequate upon retirement nearly seven years earlier,
were almost entirely dissipated due to the expenses of his
illness, his inability actively to pursue his accounting
business, a dependent wife and several seemingly safe
investments which had suffered tremendously in the
1929-1932 bear market smash. His depleted financial
condition, his developing fascination with the stock
market, and his undeniably important discoveries
combined to prompt Elliott's decision to undertake a new
profession. He decided to "begin all over again," as he put
it, "especially in work which I like, which is half the
battle." So, at the age of 64, Elliott launched his new
career and started what he later referred to as "Wave
Number five of my own life."

Spreading the Word

By November 1934, the application of Elliott's
theories was developed to the point that he decided to
present them to at least one member of the financial
community. For quite some time Elliott had subscribed to
a market service founded and edited by Charles J. Collins
and published by Investment Counsel, Inc. (later Investment Letters, Inc.) of Detroit. He was particularly
impressed by it. Elliott felt that he had learned enough
about Charles Collins through his stock market publication to trust him with his discovery. This assumption, to
Elliott's great advantage, proved correct.

On December 2, 1934, Collins, President of

Investment Counsel, received from Elliott a letter* marked "PERSONAL and CONFIDENTIAL" dated November 28. Therein Elliott explained that he had discovered three novel features of market action, recognition of wave termination, classification of wave degree, and time forecasting, which were "a much needed compliment to the Dow Theory." He even forecasted that the market advance then unfolding would be followed not by a correction, as had been the case with the two previous legs of advance, but by "a major bear collapse." (This is exactly what happened later, as the dramatic market collapse in 1937-38 erased 50% of the market's value in less than twelve months.)

Elliott asked Collins to finance a trip to Detroit so that he could present his theories completely to him, in hopes that Collins would decide to use the technique of the Wave Principle in his stock market letter to their mutual benefit. Elliott even commented that Collins, if he preferred to keep it secret, need not inform his readers that he was using the Wave Principle as a basis for his investment advice.

Collins was intrigued, but not convinced. He filed Elliott's letter and returned a standard response to the effect that he would be happy to monitor Elliott's "calls" on the market, by telegram collect or by air mail letter, for one complete market cycle to see if they had any real merit. If they proved accurate, then he would consider further steps.

Collins had developed this method of putting off the numerous "geniuses" who continually offered him "foolproof" systems for beating the market, on the assumption that any truly worthwhile system would stand out when applied in current time. Not surprisingly, the vast majority of these systems proved to be dismal failures. Elliott's principle, however, was another story.

Although Collins assured Elliott he need not divulge his method, Elliott began sending Collins a series

* This letter is reproduced in Elliott Wave Principle -- Key To Stock Market Profits (New Classics Library, 1978).

of letters and charts outlining the basis of what he referred to variously as "wave theory" or the "Five Wave Principle." Elliott stressed that since his financial status was difficult, he wished to acquaint Collins with the theory and prove its value without waiting two or more years for a complete market cycle.

Included with Elliott's second letter to Collins dated December 9, 1934, was a brief but thorough exposition of the Wave Principle, including an introduction, which constituted the first words Elliott ever wrote to another on his theory of the stock market:

The market may be likened to a river. It has rather well defined borders of uniform width, occasionally becomes blocked by barriers and suddenly breaks away from them. When the channel is narrow the speed is greater and vice versa. It curves according to resistance.

Elliott made it clear that he also used fixed-time cycles in his analysis at that time, and referred specifically to a nine week cycle, variable to twelve weeks, which is still quite regular even today.

Elliott's interest in numbers, their properties, and any apparent connection to human affairs was keen even at this early date, as the following passage from his second letter demonstrates:

360 degrees divided by ⌊2⌋ continuously will produce a number whose units always add to 9 or multiples of 9:

$$360/2 = 180; \quad 1 + 8 + 0 = 9$$
$$180/2 = 90; \quad 9 + 0 = 9$$
$$90/2 = 45; \quad 4 + 5 = 9$$
$$45/2 = 22.5; \quad 2 + 2 + 5 = 9$$
$$22.5/2 = 11.25; \quad 1 + 1 + 2 + 5 = 9$$
$$11.25/2 = 5.625; \quad 5 + 6 + 2 + 5 = 18, \text{ etc.}$$

Each degree is composed of 60 minutes, and each minute is composed of 60 seconds. The circle is subdivided into 6 equal segments, i.e. 60, 120, 180, 240, 300 and 360 degrees. The digits of each of these add to 9 or multiples of 3. The circle was also divided

[by the Babylonians] into four segments or seasons.
From 0 to 90, 90 to 180, 180 to 270 and 270 to 360.
The digits of each of these adds 9. Further subdividing the circle into eighths gives degrees as follows:
0, 45, 90, 135, 180, 225, 270, 315 and 360; the digits
of all add 9.

The first line of the square, from 1 to 90, prefaces a
reversal, i.e., the second line of the square, 90 to
180. When the four sides are completed, a complete
reversal is forecasted by wave No. 5, which is the
centre around which everything revolves.

All life and movement consists of vibrations and the
stock market is no exception.

Elliott's letters revealed a firm belief in the
virtue of individual initiative and a recognition of the
harm of government intervention. One letter referred to
the "unprecedented unconstitutional meddling in economics by politics." In another, he discussed the plight of
the railroads, with which he was undoubtedly familiar
from experience:

I see little or no hope of activity in durable goods so
long as Regimentation is displacing Individualism.
But for Individualism there would never have been
anything to regiment. The rails have been in a
secular decline since 1906 [when] politicians and
labor unions combined to harass them. The Utilities
are getting their dose of politics now; their treatment is reflected in the averages to the sorrow of
thousands of innocent investors.

During this letter writing period, Elliott
continued to discover new tenets of the Wave Principle as
his studies grew more thorough. While previously
attempting to count five waves in every movement, for
instance, he came to conclude that all "triangles, periods
of hesitation, flats, are equivalent to 'corrections' of the
ruling trend." Later he found that "diagonal triangles are
inevitable terminations of movements of their degree."

Since Collins was in Florida that winter as was
his custom, it was not until January 4, 1935 that he began

responding to Elliott's "flood of letters," as Elliott himself put it, a task which had until then been left to an associate. On January 11, Collins sent a telegram to Elliott asking him to dispatch a wire when a particular minor declining wave they were tracking had ended.

A week later the Dow Jones averages were still in a declining phase and as Elliott put it, "the wiseacres around here are very bearish." At that time he was forecasting that the Rails would break their 1934 low but the Industrials would not, a prediction which must have struck Collins later as uncannily accurate. His first telegram in response to Collins' request for pinpointing the bottom of the correction was dated January 15, 1935 and read, CORRECTION ENDED LAST HALF HOUR TODAY. The call was perfect, and a rally ensued immediately. On January 22, Elliott recognized the rally as a corrective wave advance, and after the close wrote to say, "the picture is bearish again." The rally peaked two trading hours later. He then forecast that the Dow would slip below 99 to 96 and the rails would crack 33 as larger waves 3, 4 and 5 downward unfolded.

Most of the predictions which Elliott made in his barrage of letters (even those which took years to prove) were correct, many to perfection. However, in the approach to the actual bottom, which was made at 96 as Elliott first forecast, he changed his mind several times in an attempt to call the bottom exactly to the hour. Elliott's changes of mind, newly discovered tenets, and occasional wave re-labeling bothered Collins, who wrote Elliott a long and courteous letter on February 15 pointing out weaknesses in Elliott's methods and enclosing some of his own work on a five wave theory as applied to long term price movements. He also suggested that, in order to remedy his financial situation, Elliott manage some risk capital and begin a letter service to be circulated to a select group while he developed his theories to completion. He also offered to introduce Elliott to Robert Rhea.

Elliott responded rather impishly by listing the various imperfections in Collins' own market letter's investment decisions of the previous two years. He also reaffirmed his wish to become associated with Collins, whose letters, he stated, were so well done that there was "no comparison between your letters and those of any other service that I have ever seen."

On February 19, 1935, Elliott mailed Collins seventeen pages of a somewhat unorganized yet meticulously detailed treatise entitled "The Wave Principle." Twelve more pages and five additional charts were sent over the next two months along with Elliott's regular correspondence. The first page of the treatise contains Elliott's statement of the utility of the Wave Principle:

A careful study of certain recurring phenomena within the price structure itself has developed certain facts which, while they are not always vocal, do nevertheless furnish a principle that determines the trend and gives clear warning of reversal.

Collins began to write Elliott more frequently at this point, and sent him several books, book recommendations and articles of interest, including "The Relation of Phyllotaxis to Mechancial Laws" (Oxford, 1901, 1903), a pamphlet by Professor A.H. Church of Oxford University, and fascinating excerpts from Jeans' The Mysterious Universe (1930). In the excerpt from Jeans' book, Collins included the following quotation:

From the broad philosophical standpoint, the outstanding achievement of twentieth century physics is not the theory of relativity with its welding together of space and time, or the theory of quanta with its present apparent negation of the laws of causation, or the dissection of the atom with the resultant discovery that things are not what they seem; it is the general recognition that we are not yet in contact with ultimate reality. To borrow Locke's phrase, "the real essence of substances" is forever unknowable. We can only progress by discussing the laws which govern the changes of substances, and so produce the phenomena of the external world.

In referring to the repetition of five waves in the stock market, Elliott responded, "Possibly the reason why I have not yet, and possibly never will know why this series occurs is because it is a law of nature. The laws of nature, and incidentally economics, are ruthless, which is as it should be."

Most importantly, the material Collins sent introduced Elliott to the concept of Fibonacci numbers and their relationship to natural phenomena. These excerpts undoubtedly provided the spark needed for Elliott's theories to gel into their final form.

Collins' justifiable skepticism concerning Elliott's methods was completely dispelled with the next occurrence. The Dow Jones averages had been declining throughout early 1935, and Elliott had been pinpointing hourly turns with a fair degree of accuracy. In the second week of February, the Dow Jones Rail Average, as Elliott had predicted, broke below its 1934 low of 33.19. Advisors were turning negative and memories of the 1929-32 crash were immediately rekindled as bearish pronouncements about the future course of the economy proliferated. The Dow Industrials had fallen about eleven per cent and were approaching the 96 level while the Rails, from their 1933 peak, had fallen almost fifty per cent to the 27 level.

On Wednesday, March 13, 1935, just after the close of trading with the Dow finishing near the lows for the day, Elliott sent his famous telegram to Collins and flatly stated the following: "NOTWITHSTANDING BEARISH (DOW) IMPLICATIONS ALL AVERAGES ARE MAKING FINAL BOTTOM."

Collins read the telegram on the morning of the very next day, Thursday, March 14, 1935, the day which marked the final closing low for the Dow Industrial Average. The day previous to the telegram, Tuesday, March 12, had marked the final closing low for the Dow Jones Rails.

The precise hourly low for the Industrials occurred at 11:00 on the opening of the following Monday, thirteen trading hours after Elliott's telegram was sent, with the Rails holding above their prior low. The opening selling pushed the Dow just pennies below the closing low on Thursday and a hair's breadth above Elliott's target at the 96 level. The thirteen month corrective wave was over and the market turned immediately to the upside.

Two months later, Elliott's "call" had been proved so precisely and dramatically correct as the market continued on its upward climb that Collins, "impressed by his dogmatism and accuracy," wrote and proposed that Investment Counsel, Inc. subscribe for payment to Elliott's forecasts and commented, "we are of the opinion that the Wave Principle is by far the best forecasting 'approach' that has come to our attention."

Elliott responded with a proposal that Collins subscribe to his market timing service for a period of two years. Then, if Investment Counsel was still satisfied with Elliott's success after the two year period, Collins, whom Elliott considered a master writer, would prepare a book on the Wave Principle suitable for public distribution. Elliott stipulated that the book should carry Collins' name as author, but that Elliott was to be given full credit for the discovery and development of the Wave Principle. The copyright was to be in both their names. Elliott apparently felt that Collins' name would be useful in giving the book a wider acceptance. He added that if Collins wished, he would have the option to substitute Elliott's name as author but would forfeit any claim to copyright as a result.

Collins accepted Elliott's terms and invited Elliott to Michigan to be his personal house guest for three days over a weekend in the summer of 1935. Elliott went over his theory in greater detail and thoroughly familiarized Collins with the working details of the Wave Principle.

For the next two years, as per their agreement, Collins received and monitored Elliott's calls on the market. His accuracy remained true, and at the end of the second year, in March 1937, he began working on Elliott's first monograph, The Wave Principle, based partly on Elliott's original treatise.

The Road to Wall Street

By this time Elliott was so involved with the Wave Principle that he insisted that if he were to be taken into Collins' organization, Investment Counsel's stock market service would have to use his approach exclusively, a proposal which Collins could not accept. However, in appreciation of Elliott's decision to confide to him the details of the Wave Principle, and in fulfillment of their agreement, Collins completed <u>The Wave Principle</u>, which was published formally on August 31, 1938. The 8 1/2" x 11" monograph was printed in dark blue softcover with no cover markings. An estimated five hundred copies were printed.

Elliott then packed up his belongings and moved with his wife to Brooklyn Heights, New York, a brief subway stop from Manhattan's financial district, to launch his new career. Collins graciously provided Elliott some financial assistance, referred to him a number of discretionary accounts, and helped him set up his office at 25

The Standish Arms Hotel (note the bust of Miles Standish on the facade), 169 Columbia Heights, Brooklyn, New York. Elliott's home from 1938(?) to 1947. Photo 1990 by Paul Brodtkorb.

Broad Street, where Elliott began managing some speculative funds for several well-to-do clients. Then on November 10, three months after The Wave Principle was released, Elliott published the first in a long series of Interpretive Letters.* Elliott initially priced his Interpretive Letters at $60 per year and continued to make available his monograph, which he called "the Treatise," for $15.

Collins had counseled Elliott against overly publicizing his findings, but Elliott considered it a necessary step and insisted on it. Several months later, at Elliott's urging, Collins, who had been writing regular feature articles for Financial World magazine, contacted the editors and introduced them to Elliott and his work. In 1939, Elliott was commissioned by Financial World to write twelve articles on the Wave Principle. After their "announcement" on March 29, the first of Elliott's articles appeared in the April 5 issue and their publication continued regularly into July. These definitive articles established Elliott's reputation with the investment community. They had great staying power and survived in various forms over the years, while the monographs were never reprinted.

Elliott's Interpretive Letters outlined and forecasted the path of the market in terms of the Wave Principle. He issued the one to four page letters irregularly ("as the occasion requires"), ranging from three to seven issues per year between November 10, 1938 and August 6, 1945. In late 1939, after the publication of the Financial World articles, Elliott began writing in depth follow-up essays on various aspects of the Wave Principle. These quickly evolved into a formal Educational Service, which he published from 1940 to 1944, and for which he charged $60 per year. With this service, he expanded upon his monograph and articles as he came across new observations and ideas. Titles included "Technical Features," "Alternation," "The Basis of the Wave Principle,"

---

* All known copies have been republished, along with a Foreword providing a more complete discussion of his services, in R. N. Elliott's Market Letters, 1938-1945 (New Classics Library, 1991).

"Duration or Time Element," "Inflation," "Dynamic Symmetry", "Two Cycles of American History," "The Law of Motion" and "Nature's Law" (a precursor to his second monograph).

Elliott's other services included:

-- Forecast Letters, marked "Confidential" and sold at "conventional fees." These one page bulletins provided investment timing recommendations "for those who desire prompt advice when important reversals are due in averages and individual stocks."

-- Special reports for "business executives" designed to be of help in detecting "peaks and nadirs of production."

-- A service called "Information," whereby non-subscribers were allowed to send a stamped self addressed envelope and ask Elliott any question about the Wave Principle. Elliott responded with a quotation of the fee he required for his response, and upon payment, the answer. "This novel service," said Elliott, "fills a long felt need."

-- He even designed a 61.8% ruler,* probably created using a drafting instrument called a "proportional divider," the fulcrum of which can be moved to obtain different ratios of measurement. Elliott's handy ruler enabled the user to ascertain without the bother of calculation when the ratio between two lengths was 61.8%. Elliott offered it for sale at 25 cents.

Elliott said in 1935 that "waves do not make errors, but my version may be defective. [However], the nearer one approaches the primary law, the less errors will occur." By virtue of all his painstaking study, Elliott rightly considered himself the sole authority on his discovery. Toward the establishment of that position, he

---

* A picture of the ruler is shown in R. N. Elliott's Market Letters, 1938-1945 (New Classics Library, 1991).

delivered the following warning on the front page of The Wave Principle:

> When a newly discovered phenomenon is disclosed, self-appointed 'experts' immediately appear. Considerable experience is required to interpret correctly waves which are in process of formation. No interpretation of the Wave Principle should be accepted as valid unless made by me or by a student directly licensed by me.

In fact, Elliott did have a class of students whom he taught at irregular intervals from his small office at 25 Broad Street. Carroll Gianni, a member of the New York Stock Exchange, was an occasional student of Elliott's during 1939. He describes the one-hour sessions as informal but Socratic in style, with Elliott firmly in the role of "teacher."

In the spring of 1942, Elliott moved his office to 63 Wall Street through an interesting chain of events. Philip K. Sweet, then president of Fundamental Investors, Inc., had worked for Edgar Lawrence Smith in the latter 1920s with Anthony Gaubis, who in 1934 became associated as a junior partner with Charles J. Collins at Investment Counsel, Inc. in Detroit. Gaubis had met Elliott in 1938 at Investment Counsel and later introduced him to Sweet in New York. Sweet, who admired Elliott's work, offered him an office at 63 Wall Street where Fundamental Investors was located. Elliott accepted, and moved his business from 25 Broad Street to his new location.

Elliott licensed at least one student of whom there is some record, a man named Richard Martin who published four market letters entitled "The Wave Principle" from March to August, 1942. Elliott made certain to protect his discovery even from his proteges, and had the letters copyrighted in his own name. Mr. Martin's career with Elliott was brief, however, possibly because he found himself in disagreement with Elliott on the outlook for the market. Interpretations of the status of the market under the Wave Principle are often open to various alternatives. While Elliott was always glad to discuss different points of view, he saw his interpretations

63 Wall Street, New York. Elliott's office location from 1942 to 1947(8). Photo 1990 by Robert R. Prechter, Jr.

25 Broad Street, New York. Elliott's office location from 1938 to 1942. Photo 1990 by Robert R. Prechter, Jr.

of the Wave Principle as the most expert and allowed no deviations unless he authorized them. His interpretations and forecasts were usually dogmatic, and later in his life, not always as correct as he expected them to be (though almost always better than the competition). Mr. Martin dropped from view and then appeared again in 1943, author of a booklet called "Trend Action, A New Method of Forecasting." The booklet proposed an analysis of the market in a fashion similar to Elliott's but purported to be refined from a system developed by a man named Frank H. Tubbs and published in 1929 as part of a course entitled "Tubbs Analytics." It was once suggested that Tubbs was annoyed that Elliott had exploited "his" discovery. However, surviving literature of Tubbs' clearly fails to indicate anything but a superficial similarity to Elliott's Wave Principle, thus dismissing any claim of theft.

Elliott may well have been a victim of theft, however. In October 1940, Elliott published his very first discussion of "The Fibonacci Summation Series of Dynamic Symmetry" and its relationship to the Wave Principle in a treatise entitled "The Basis of the Wave Principle."* Shortly thereafter, on May 19, 1941, appeared an article by "Edson Beers" in Barron's. "Edson Beers" in fact was a pseudonym of Edson Gould, whose middle name was Beers. The article, "Applying the Principles of Dynamic Symmetry to the Stock Market," purported to introduce this unquestionably novel idea yet neglected to mention Elliott, its original and foremost proponent. Gould confirmed that the editor of Barron's told him he had received a call from Elliott, who was (justifiably) angry about the article. Whether Gould got the ideas directly from Elliott's writings is unclear. Gould would not comment on this question, although he inaccurately recollected that his article appeared in March 1935, thus pre-dating Elliott's work when in fact it was published six years later. At minimum, it certainly can be said that in late 1940 and early 1941, due to Elliott's publications, discussion of these ideas was in the air. Gould later used Elliott's principles, restated in general terms, plus his own indicators and calculations,

---

* Republished in R. N. Elliott's Market Letters, 1938-1945 (New Classics Library, 1991).

to make some of the most brilliantly accurate long term forecasts in stock market history. While Elliott's Wave Principle never got credit for Gould's forecasts, it clearly should have received a great deal.

Branching Out

As his career progressed, Elliott began to expand his scope of interests beyond the stock market. He had always applied the Wave Principle to data series outside the stock market, and had for quite some time connected the phenomenon with the Fibonacci sequence. However, he had yet to attempt to define the broader meaning of the Wave Principle and its connection with the natural laws of the universe. It was during the early 1940s that Elliott developed to completion his concept that the rhythmical ebb and flow of human emotions and activities followed a natural progression governed by universal laws of nature, laws which had been known for centuries by great philosophers, scientists, artists, architects and mathematicians, and which, not surprisingly, were revered by mystics.

From early 1940 onward, Elliott began investigating further in the fields of philosophy, art, dynamic symmetry, Egyptology and pyramidology, mathematics, physics and botany. He read Count N. Boncampagni's publication of Fibonacci's works, two books on the subject of Dynamic Symmetry by Jay Hambidge, an American artist who until his death in 1924 applied the principles of geometry to art and architecture in several books, Nature's Harmonic Unity and Proportional Form, both by Samuel Coleman and C. Arthur Coan, Curves of Light by Thomas A. Cook (supplied to him by Collins in 1935), "Emotional Cycles of Individuals," an article in Red Book on the work of Dr. Rexford B. Hersey, a scientist who discovered the cyclicality of human emotions (today called biorhythms), Prophecies of Melchi-Zedik in the Great Pyramid, by Brown Landone, Life's Riddle Solved (1945) by Dr. John H. Manas, president of the Pythagorean Society, and other volumes as well, some of which are listed in the "References" section at the end of Nature's Law. More and more, his concept took on a wholeness which fit into what he eventually came to call "Nature's

Law" or "The Secret of the Universe."

Some time prior to 1944, Elliott corresponded with Manly P. Hall, head of the Philosophical Society of Los Angeles. Elliott requested permission to reprint the picture of Pythagoras that Hall had contributed to John H. Manas' book. Permission was granted and Elliott reproduced the picture on page 58 of Nature's Law. Hall, who chronicled man's search for the secret of "Universal Wisdom," and who maintained that "all the universe is eternal growth," may have influenced Elliott's thinking by the time he wrote Nature's Law.

During these years, Elliott visited investment counselor George P. Robinson almost daily in his offices at 14 Wall Street. Robinson employee Howard Fay became friends with Elliott, whom he visited several times in Brooklyn and whom he described as "intelligent and sharp." He was "ornery at times," though, says Fay, and less than patient with those who disagreed with him.

By 1945, Elliott was established to the point that he was advertising for Graphics Stocks, a monthly range chart service published and updated every two months. Obviously his students needed charts, and F. W. Stephens, the distributor, felt Elliott could supply him some business by recommending them as ideal for illustrating the principle of wave movement. Annual subscriptions sold for $50.

How ironic it seems that the owner of a challenging market analysis business and a man of increasingly expansive philosophical thoughts would take the time to write a dry practical booklet, based on his earlier career as an accountant, entitled "Farm Tax Accounting As You Go," published in January, 1945. It is as if, with only a few years left to live, Elliott was not only branching out in several avenues of investigation and thought, but finishing projects long planned yet previously left undone.

The Final Years

During the last three years of his life, Elliott's clients continued to call him, mostly for advice on the very short term moves in the market. However, he ceased to solicit new business. Elliott wrote the last of his Interpretive Letters in August 1945 and spent the rest of the year and the first five months of 1946 putting together what he obviously considered his definitive work, Nature's Law -- The Secret of the Universe. Nature's Law incorporates part of The Wave Principle and includes the additional discoveries and observations which had been detailed in his Educational and Interpretive Letters. This final monograph includes almost every thought that Elliott ever had concerning the theory of the Wave Principle, right up to the final year of his career.

The reader of that volume should keep in mind that Elliott was a pioneer. Much of his discovery was recorded at the same time it was formulated, and little time was available to be spent on cosmetics. Thus, despite its great contribution, Nature's Law was compiled haphazardly, denying the book the cohesive quality that better planning would have provided. Many of the pages were inserted directly from those Educational Letters which explored aspects of the Wave Principle developed in the years after his first monograph was published. Though Elliott brought the excitement of his discovery to the fore with many passages of brilliance and innovative energy, the difference in writing style and organization between the first monograph and the second prompted Hamilton Bolton to remark that "if one is fortunate enough to have both the first book and Elliott's later Nature's Law, one cannot but be impressed with the clarity and precision of the presentation of the first as compared to the dif-fuseness (albeit interspersed with fascinating if esoteric ideas) of the second."

It is my opinion that the second monograph suffered from diffuseness partly because of Elliott's advancing age. His earlier book on restaurant accounting was extremely well organized and presented. The Financial World articles, which Elliott most definitely wrote himself, are concise and well written, as are most of his Interpretive and Educational Letters. At seventy-five years of age and still suffering chronically from anemia, however, Elliott may have felt a sense of urgency about getting his ideas into print, an urgency which took precedence over a well organized text. Perhaps in an effort to get the book out before age and ill health finally caught up with him, Elliott sacrificed meticulous organization for speed and thoroughness.

The publication date of the book was June 10, 1946. It was printed in an 8 1/2" x 11" buff colored softcover ring binder, and the reported 1,000 copies sold out quickly to various members of the New York financial community. While a copy of The Wave Principle and of each market letter Elliott wrote were meticulously sent to the Library of Congress, Elliott apparently neglected to send a copy of Nature's Law.

Elliott lost his wife soon after the publication of Nature's Law. His only relatives, it appears, were a niece and nephew in Los Angeles, the latter an asthma sufferer. Howard Fay described Elliott as becoming quite lonely in his apartment at the Standish Arms Hotel, 169 Columbia Heights, Brooklyn. Less than a year afterward, Elliott's Wall Street friends convinced him to move out of his hotel suite. These same friends probably financed Elliott's move to one of New York's leading hospitals for the mentally ill, a type of facility which in those days also served as a home for the elderly. There Elliott's basic needs were satisfied as he lived out the final months of his life. According to accounts, he remained as mentally energetic as ever. Elliott and Collins continued their occasional meetings, and remained friends and corres- pondents until Elliott's death on January 15, 1948. One former trader claims that a collection was taken up among friends for Elliott's cremation, which took place two days later at the Fairchild Funeral Home in Brooklyn. In reviewing the records on file there, a representative remarked that in all her years at the facility, she had hardly seen a sketchier record, the few details provided by his otherwise unidentified niece from Los Angeles. An obituary ran in The New York Times.

The Wave Principle After Elliott

After Elliott's death, none of his students attempted to take over his publication where he left off. However, the idea was just too powerful to be allowed to fade into obscurity. In fact, with great success, it was adopted and utilized by three of the greatest thinkers in the history of the market analysis: Edson Gould (see p. 26), E. George Schaefer and A. Hamilton Bolton.

Dow Theory expert E. George Schaefer knew R. N. Elliott, and began publishing the Dow Theory Trader (1948-1974) the year Elliott died. He incorporated Elliott's ideas into his analysis, and became one of the most successful market forecasters ever. Thus, just as one Dow Theorist (Robert Rhea) had provided inspiration to Elliott, who began publishing the year after Rhea died, so Elliott provided inspiration to Schaefer, in effect returning the favor. However, it was Hamilton Bolton, the brilliant analyst of Bolton-Tremblay, Ltd. of Montreal, who truly kept the Wave Principle alive. Bolton had read Elliott's Financial World articles in the spring and summer months of 1939* and made a point of contacting Elliott on one or two occasions on his trips to New York. They continued correspondence until Elliott's death, but it was not until five years later in 1953 that Bolton decided to assume the task of publicly analyzing the market in terms of what was by then referred to as the "Elliott" Wave Principle.

Bolton commanded great respect within the investment community because of his pioneering work on the relationship of bank credit statistics to stock market behavior. His lucid, thoughtful commentary and dramatic success with the Wave Principle kept Wall Street interested in the concept for fourteen years. Bolton first expressed his thoughts on the Wave Principle and its implications for the future path of the market in a 1953 supplement to the Bank Credit Analyst, which he edited. His analysis proved popular enough that the Elliott Wave Supplement became an annual feature published each April.** Elliott's Wave Principle got another small boost with the inclusion of a concise summary in Garfield Drew's

---

* Bolton, in a Supplement to the Bank Credit Analyst, erroneously referred to their publication as the summer and fall months of 1938.
** All of these have been republished in The Elliott Wave Writings of A. Hamilton Bolton (New Classics Library, 1991).

1955 book, <u>New Methods for Profit in the Stock Market</u>.
In it, Drew commented as follows:

> After a brave start in 1949-1951, the past two years,
> at least, have detracted from long term 1948 fore-
> casts of most basic cycles. If these projections had
> been correct, stocks should have reached a bear
> market low in 1951, building activity should have
> been on the downgrade until 1953, and 1951-1952
> should have been the trough of a depression. There is
> one exception, however. Elliott's Wave Principle
> seems to have stood up better than anything else in
> the field of long range forecast. There was more
> hesitation of stock prices in 1947-1949 than originally
> anticipated, but the basic theory was quite correct
> that the next important move would not only be up,
> but would also exceed the 1946 top. At the same
> time, it was also forecast that, eventually, a fifth
> "wave" would exceed even the 1928-29 top for stock
> prices. That seemed utterly fantastic in 1948 when
> the 200 level would have looked "high," but with the
> Average having already hit 360 in 1954, it no longer
> appears quite so impossible of ultimate accomplish-
> ment.

In 1960, Bolton wrote <u>The Elliott Wave
Principle -- a Critical Appraisal</u>,* the first book on the
Wave Principle since Elliott's own Nature's Law. In that
volume, he made his famous prediction forecasting a
major Dow peak at 999, reached six years later almost to
the dollar. He also documented, without referring to him
by name, Collins' concept of a 1932 orthodox Supercycle
low for stocks, Elliott's concept of a 1942 orthodox low
based on a 13-year triangle, and his own re-interpretation
of a 1949 orthodox low based on a 21-year triangle. These
differences of opinion constituted what was probably the
most enduring controversy among students of the Wave
Principle. A. J. Frost recounts that Bolton, just months
before his death, changed his mind on the 21-year triangle
and adopted the concept of the 1932 orthodox low, clearly
the best wave count given subsequent market action.

On Wednesday, February 11, 1966, two days

---

* See previous footnote.

after that decade's high and the peak of Cycle Wave III, Bolton wrote Collins, whom he had met twice before, and asked him to contribute to the Bank Credit Analyst's 1966 Supplement. Therein Collins gave his thoughts on the market and explained the story of his relationship with R. N. Elliott. In this early 1966 Supplement, Collins, after outlining the Intermediate, Primary, Cycle, Supercycle and even Grand Supercycle wave counts for the stock market, correctly identified the top of the huge extended Cycle wave advance from 1942. At the same time he called for an ensuing fourth wave to be made up of a very large A-B-C formation carrying ultimately to about the 525 level on the Dow. Considering that the Dow at that time was close to 1000 and bears were few and far between, Collins' prediction was truly remarkable, not only because it forecast the unthinkable, but because it came true. The end of the 1966-1974 correction envisaged by Collins came at 570 on the Dow, just 45 points from the projection made eight years earlier.

A. J. Frost, as vice president in charge of administration at Bolton-Tremblay, was a business associate of Bolton's from 1960 to 1962. After his departure, Frost remained one of Bolton's closest friends. They corresponded frequently and discussed in detail the market and the Wave Principle on many occasions. After Bolton's death on April 5, 1967, Frost was chosen to assume the task of writing the Elliott Wave Supplements. Frost wrote the 1967 Supplement and collaborated with Russ Hall on the 1968 Supplement. The last Elliott Wave publication issued by the Bank Credit Analyst, which had been purchased by Storey, Boeckh & Associates following Bolton's death, was Frost's 1970 Supplement, which included his famous calculation that the bear market then in progress would bottom at 572. The actual hourly low four years later was 572.20.

The Wave Principle then dropped from public view except for the appearance of minor additions to the literature, usually articles or book chapters. Most references to the Wave Principle were a re-hash of previous material, with the notable exception of R. C. Beckman's The Elliott Wave Principle as Applied to the London Stock Market (1976), the most ambitious work on the subject during this period.

The Wave Principle Renewed

The Elliott silence wasn't broken decisively until the release of Frost's and my 1978 book, ELLIOTT WAVE PRINCIPLE -- KEY TO STOCK MARKET PROFITS, the first book both to arrange all known aspects of the Wave Principle in logical sequence and to add points of substance to the literature.

In late 1976, while I was still a technical analyst with Merrill Lynch in New York, I began correspondence with A. J. Frost. I had been publishing reports on the status of the market in terms of the Wave Principle and was beginning research for a new book on Elliott. The Market Technicians' Association contacted me in early 1977 and asked me to arrange for Frost to speak at their annual conference in Pennsylvania that May.

When Frost and I met at the conference, we enjoyed each other's company immensely and became fast friends. Frost explained that he also was in the process of writing a book on Elliott, which was to be a collaborative effort with Ian McAvity of Deliberations (for artwork) and Richard Russell of Dow Theory Letters. Like Schaefer, Russell, today's leading Dow Theorist, often utilized Elliott Wave interpretations in his stock market service. Frost added that he would like to include some of my recent analytical work in a chapter. I agreed, and began work on the chapter, while continuing research on my own book.

Frost spent most of 1977 writing a draft of his book, which I expressed an interest in seeing. Then, late in that year, both McAvity and Russell contacted Frost and explained that their busy schedules precluded their involvement with the book. Frost wrote and suggested we collaborate on the volume, and in December invited me for a weekend to his home in Manotick, Ontario to go over our plans. I then spent the next seven months expanding on AJ's draft, interrupted only by a delightful weekend visit with Frost and Collins at Collins' retreat in Florida. By July the book was completed. The next several weeks were devoted to production details such as drawing the illustrations, then photographing them and developing the photos in the basement darkroom at the house of market analysis pioneer Arthur Merrill. By August the manuscript was at the printers and in November it was released.

In April 1979 I left my position as a Technical Market Specialist with Merrill Lynch and began publishing THE ELLIOTT WAVE THEORIST, which I hope will track the fifth wave in the current Supercycle as well as Elliott tracked the first and second, as Bolton tracked the third and Frost the fourth (and as Collins has tracked them all).

In 1979 I began assembling THE MAJOR WORKS OF R.N. ELLIOTT. The result is this volume, which I hope has left no stone unturned in helping make available to R. N. Elliott the wide audience his pioneering ideas so richly deserve.

--- Robert R. Prechter, Jr., 1979

THE WAVE PRINCIPLE
by
R.N. ELLIOTT

PUBLISHERS' NOTE: In the original printing of The Wave Principle, most of the charts and diagrams were placed in the back of the book. For easier reference, we have re-arranged their placement to appear within the text where reference is made to them.

---

[1] (See opposite page.) What Elliott meant was that no rallies in the few years following publication in 1938 would develop into five-wave bull markets, since a bear market of Cycle degree was still in progress from 1937. He was absolutely correct. No "bull market" occurred until 1942-1946.

THE WAVE PRINCIPLE

by

R. N. ELLIOTT,

Discoverer.

Permission has been granted the author
to reproduce charts prepared by:

E. W. Axe & Co.,
Standard Statistics Co. Inc.,
New York Stock Exchange,
Barrons, The National Financial Weekly.
Dow-Jones & Co., Inc.

Numbering and lettering of waves was done
by the author and is protected by copyright.

Warning: When a newly discovered phenomenon is disclosed,
self-appointed "experts" immediately appear.

Considerable experience is required to interpret
correctly waves which are in process of formation.

Long distance forecasting requires thorough
familiarity with historical precedent.   During [1]
the next few years the market will not follow
the pattern observed between 1932 and 1937.

No interpretation of the Wave Principle should be
accepted as valid unless made by me or by a student
directly licensed by me.

R. N. Elliott.

New York.

I

RHYTHM IN NATURE

No truth meets more general acceptance than that the universe is ruled by law. Without law it is self-evident there would be chaos, and where chaos is, nothing is. Navigation, chemistry, aeronautics, architecture, radio transmission, surgery, music -- the gamut, indeed, of art and science -- all work, in dealing with things animate and things inanimate, under law because nature herself works in this way. Since the very character of law is order, or constancy, it follows that all that happens will repeat and can be predicted if we know the law.

Columbus, maintaining that the world was round, predicted that a westward course from Europe must eventually bring his ships to land and despite scoffers, even among his own crew, saw his prediction realized. Halley, calculating the orbit of the 1682 comet, predicted its return which was strikingly verified in 1759. Marconi, after his studies in electrical transmission, predicted that sound could be conveyed without wires, and today we can sit in our homes and listen to musical and other programs from across the ocean. These men, as have countless more in other fields, learned the law. After becoming thus posted, prediction was easy because it became mathematical.

Even though we may not understand the cause underlying a particular phenomenon, we can, by observation, predict that phenomenon's recurrence. The sun was expected to recurrently rise at a fixed time thousands of years before the cause operating to produce this result was known. Indians fix their month by each new moon, but even today cannot tell why regular intervals characterize this heavenly sign. Spring plantings are witnessed the world over because summer is expected as next in order; yet how many planters understand why they are afforded this constancy of the seasons? In each instance the rhythm of the particular phenomenon was mastered.

Man is no less a natural object than the sun or

the moon, and his actions, too, in their metrical occurrence, are subject to analysis. Human activities, while amazing in character, if approached from the rhythmical bias, contain a precise and natural answer to some of our most perplexing problems. Furthermore, because man is subject to rhythmical procedure, calculations having to do with his activites can be projected far into the future with a justification and certainty heretofore unattainable.

Very extensive research in connection with what may be termed human activities indicates that practically all developments which result from our social-economic processes follow a law that causes them to repeat themselves in similar and constantly recurring serials of waves or impulses of definite number and pattern. It is likewise indicated that in their intensity, these waves or impulses bear a consistent relation to one another and to the passage of time. In order to best illustrate and expound this phenomenon it is necessary to take, in the field of man's activities, some example which furnishes an abundance of reliable data and for such purpose there is nothing better than the stock exchange.

Particular attention has been given to the stock market for two reasons. In the first place, there is no other field in which prediction has been essayed with such great intensity and with so little result. Economists, statisticians, technicians, business leaders and bankers all have had a try at foretelling the future of prices over the New York Stock Exchange. Indeed, there has developed a definite profession with market forecasting as its objective. Yet 1929 came and went and the turn from the greatest bull market on record to the greatest bear market on record caught almost every investor off guard. Leading investment institutions, spending hundreds of thousands of dollars yearly on market research, were caught by surprise and suffered millions of dollars loss because of price shrinkage in stock holdings that were carried too long.

A second reason for choosing the stock market as an illustration of the wave impulse common to social-economic activity is the great reward attendant on successful stock market prediction. Even accidental success in some single market forecast has yielded riches little short of the fabulous. In the market advance from July 1932 to March 1937, for illustration, an average of thirty leading and representative stocks advanced by 373%. During the course of this five-year movement, however, there were individual stocks whose per cent advance was much larger. Lastly, the broad advance cited above was not in a straight upward line, but rather by a series of upward and downward steps, or zig-zag movements of a number of months' duration. These lesser swings afforded even greater opportunity for profit.

Despite the attention given the stock market, success, both in the accuracy of prediction and the bounties attendant thereto, has necessarily been haphazard becasuse those who have attempted to deal with the market's movements have failed to recognize the extent to which the market is a psychological phenomenon. They have not grasped the fact that there is regularity underlying the fluctuations of the market, or, stated otherwise, that price movements in stocks are subject to rhythms, or an ordered sequence. Thus market predictions, as those who have had any experience in the subject well know, have lacked certainty or value of any but an accidental kind.

But the market has its law, just as is true of other things throughout the universe. Were there no law, there could be no center about which prices could revolve and, therefore, no market. Instead, there would be a daily series of disorganized, confused price fluctuations without reason or order anywhere apparent. A close study of the market, however, as will be subsequently disclosed, proves that this is not the case. Rhythm, or regular, measured, and harmonious movement, is to be discerned. This law behind the market can be discovered only when the market is viewed in its proper light and then is analyzed from this approach. Simply put, the stock market is a creation of man and therefore reflects human idiosyncrasy. In the pages which follow, the law, or rhythm, to which man responds will be disclosed as registered by market movements that fluctuate in accordance with a definite wave principle.

The Wave Principle is a phenomenon that has

always functioned in every human activity. Waves of different degrees occur whether or not recording machinery is present. When the machinery described below is present, the patterns of waves are perfected and become visible to the experienced eye.

A. Extensive commercial activity represented by corporations whose ownership is widely distributed.

B. A general market-place where buyer and seller may contact quickly through representatives.

C. Reliable record and publications of transactions.

D. Adequate statistics available on all matters relating to corporations.

E. Daily high and low range charted in such a manner as will disclose the waves of all degrees as they occur.

The daily range of stock transactions was inaugurated in 1928 and the hourly record in 1932. These are necessary in order to observe the minor and minute waves, especially in fast markets.

The Wave Principle does not require confirmation by two averages. Each average, group, stock or any human activity is interpreted by its own waves. Behavior of waves has been fairly well explored but application is in its infancy.[2]

---

[2] Here Elliott suggests, correctly I think, that once one knows the Law, it is easy to recognize and follow, but it takes practice to be able to forecast the market from it. On the other hand, it is not necessary to forecast in order to trade successfully. As Elliott said in a letter to Collins, "I consider that it is far more important to KNOW when the terminals are actually reached than to forecast a 'guess'."

STOCK MARKET WAVES

Human emotions, as mentioned in the preceding discussion, are rhythmical. They move in waves of a definite number and direction. The phenomenon occurs in all human activities, whether it is business, politics, or the pursuit of pleasure. It is particularly evident in those free markets where public participation in price movements is extensive. Bond, stock and commodity price trends are therefore especially subject to examination and demonstration of the wave movement. This treatise has made use of price movements in stocks to illustrate the phenomenon, but all the principles laid down herein are equally applicable to the wave movement in every field where human endeavor is registered.

A completed movement consists of five waves. Why this should be five rather than some other number is one of the secrets of the universe. No attempt will be made to explain it, although, in passing, it might be observed that the figure five is prominent in other basic patterns of nature. Taking the human body, for example, there are five extensions from the torso -- head, two legs, two arms; five extensions from head -- two ears, two eyes, the nose; five extensions in the form of fingers, from each arm, and in the form of toes, from each leg; five physical senses -- taste, smell, sight, touch, hearing; and so the story might be repeated elsewhere. In any event, <u>five waves are basic to a completed social movement</u> and can be accepted without necessity of reasoning the matter out.

Three of the five waves that form any completed movement will be in the direction of the movement, two of the waves will be in a contrary direction. The first, third and fifth waves represent the forward impulse; the second and fourth waves, the contrary, or corrective. Stated otherwise, the odd numbered waves are in the main direction; the even numbered waves, against the main direction. This is illustrated in Figure 1.

Five waves of one dimension become the first wave of the next greater dimension or degree. As an example of this, the five waves in Figure 1 progressed

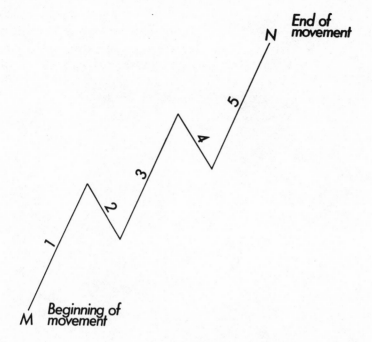

Figure 1

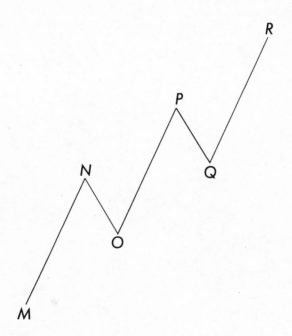

Figure 2

from point M to point N. In Figure 2, however, representing the next higher degree of movement than the one just illustrated, it will be seen that the movement from M to N is but one wave of the five-wave movement M to R. The movement M to R, in turn, becomes but the first wave of a movement of still higher degree.

IDENTIFYING THE WAVES

In the preceding discussion the wave movement in stock prices was rather generally treated, the main point established being that a movement consists of five waves, and that the five waves of one movement equal the first wave of a next higher movement. At this point a second basic fact with respect to the wave movement should be introduced. This concerns a difference between the odd numbered and the even numbered waves.

Waves one, three and five, it will be recalled, are impulses in the main direction, where waves two and four are reverse movements. Wave two serves to correct wave one, and wave four serves to correct wave three. The difference between waves in the main direction and waves against the main direction is that the former are divisible into five waves of lesser degree, whereas the latter are divisible into but three waves of the lesser degree. In the preceding discussion, the movement M to N was shown as in Figure 3.

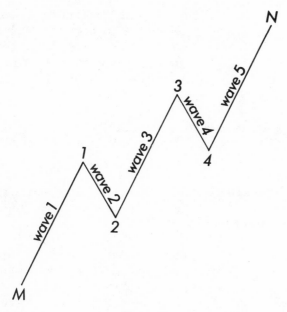

Figure 3

Were this movement also broken into waves of one lower degree, it would appear as in Figure 4.

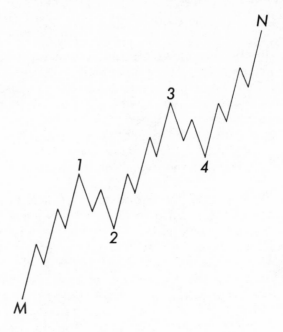

Figure 4

Note, in Figure 4, that the second wave (wave 1 to 2) and the fourth wave (wave 3 to 4) are each made up of three smaller waves, whereas waves one, three, and five each have five smaller waves. The rules to be derived from this illustration -- and these rules are fundamental to the whole wave subject -- are:

1) Waves in the direction of the main movement, or the odd numbered waves, are made up of five lesser waves.

2) Corrective waves, or waves against the main movement (even numbered waves) are made up of three lesser waves.

To further illustrate the above rules, let us take the movement 1 to 2 in Figure 4. This was wave number two of the five-wave or complete movement from M to N, and was made up, as all corrective movements should be, of three waves. The three waves of the movement 1 to 2, however, formed, when isolated, a distinct corrective movement, and, under the above rules, the odd numbered waves (or waves a and c), since they are in the

direction of the entire corrective movement 1 to 2, should
each be made up of five lesser waves, whereas the even
numbered wave (or wave b), which is against the direction
of the movement 1 to 2 and thus is a correction in such
movement, should be made up of three waves. If we now
present the movement 1 to 2 in terms of its lower waves,
it will appear as in Figure 5.

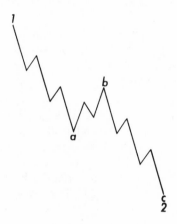

Figure 5

For purposes of convenience, let us designate
the odd numbered waves of a movement as cardinal[3]
waves and the even numbered waves as corrective waves.
Let us also remember that the cardinal waves will contain
five waves of a lower degree, whereas the corrective
waves will contain three waves of a lower degree. Other
rules and points of interest with respect to waves follow.

The wave movement applies to stock averages,
such as the Dow Jones, Standard Statistics, New York
Times; to groups of stocks, such as the steels, the coppers,
the   textiles;   and   to   individual   stocks.[4]   When

---

[3] "Cardinal" is the original term, and a good word. In
the Financial World articles, he uses the term "progressive" waves, and later in Nature's Law, "impulse" waves,
the term to which Frost and I have become accustomed.
[4] Use of the Wave Principle with individual stocks is
less reliable than with averages since the phenomenon
reflects mass psychology, or as Elliott put it, "extensive
public participation in price movements."

individual stocks are studied, it will be found that some are advancing while others are declining or undergoing a corrective movement. The great majority of individual issues will, at any given time, be following the same pattern, however, with the result that the averages, or general market, will break down into the wave phenomenon. It follows that the greater the number of stocks in a market average, the more perfect will be the wave pattern.[5]

Waves are not of uniform length or duration.[6] An entire movement, consisting of five waves, is always due to some one or more controlling influences, but the three upward waves (waves one, three, and five) which, with their two corrective waves (waves two and four), go to make up the entire movement, may accommodate themselves somewhat to current developments.[7] The fundamental cause behind such movement is generally not recognized until after the effect has played out in the form of the complete movement, whereas, during the course of the movement, current news is available to everyone and thus modifies, both as to extent and duration, each of the five waves going to make up the completed move.

---

[5] Strictly speaking, this statement is not true. An average made up of IBM and General Motors alone would better reflect the Wave Principle than an average of ten thinly traded two-dollar stocks. Moreover, I am convinced that the public visibility of a market index may enhance its utility with regard to the Wave Principle. Thus the Dow, which is made up of only thirty stocks, may be a more sensitive recorder of the Wave Principle than say, the Value Line Composite since investors have a psychological interaction with the Dow Industrial Average that they do not experience with other indexes.

[6] He means necessarily of uniform length or duration. They certainly can be, and at times are.

[7] This assertion doesn't hold true for all degrees and therefore doesn't stand up exactly as stated, since any "entire movement" is merely one of the waves of a movement of larger degree. What Elliott means is simply that news appears to affect the shape of waves of sub-minor degree.

As a general rule, it may be assumed that wave three will reach a higher level than wave one, and that wave five will go higher than wave three. Likewise, wave four should not carry to as low a level as is attained by wave two.[8] Wave two rarely cancels all of the ground gained by wave one, and wave four rarely cancels all of the ground gained by wave three.[9] The completed five-wave movement, in other words, is normally diagonal in character, as illustrated in Figure 6.

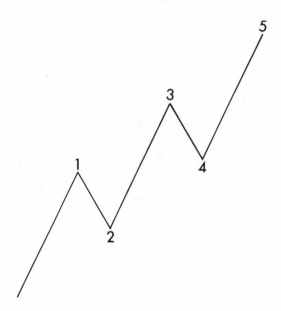

Figure 6

To properly observe a market movement, and hence to segregate the individual waves of such a movement, it is necessary that the movement, as it progresses, be channelled between parallel lines.[10] Most stationers' shops carry in stock parallel rulers and

[8] Later Elliott contended that wave 4 should not drop below the peak of wave 1, a rule with which I completely agree.
[9] If the Wave Principle is to have any consistency or value, the words "rarely" should read "never."
[10] Elliott did not claim to be the originator of the parallel system of channeling market movements, but he certainly improved upon whatever may have gone before.

the use of such a device greatly facilitates the channelling.

A channel cannot be started until waves numbers one and two have been completed. In Figure 7 waves one and two have ended, leaving three exposed contacts, or points which stand out alone. The first exposed contact is the starting point of wave number one; the second exposed contact is the termination point of wave number one as well as the starting point of wave number two; while the third exposed contact is the

Figure 7

termination point of wave number two. These points, for purposes of illustration, have been designated M, N, and O. In preparing the channel, a base line should first be drawn between exposed contacts M and O. Across exposed contact N may then be drawn a line parallel to the base line, designated as the "upper channel line." This upper channel line should be extended some distance to the right of N. When this operation has been completed, the channel will appear as in Figures 8 and 9.

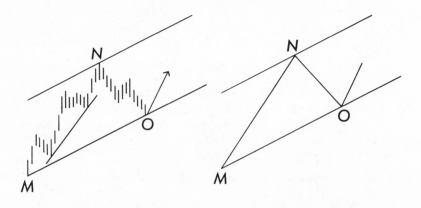

Figure 8   Figure 9

Wave number three should normally terminate at around the upper channel line. If wave number three exceeds the upper channel line, the upmovement has taken on temporary strength, whereas if wave number three terminates below the upper channel line, the upmovement has developed temporary weakness.[11] In any event, when wave three has terminated, the old channel can be abandoned in favor of a new one. The new channel is established by drawing an upper channel line to connect points N and P, or termination points of waves one and three. A line, still designated as the base line, parallel to the new upper channel line is drawn across exposed contact O and extended to the right. It is about this line that wave four should terminate. Figure 10 below shows both the old, or discarded, and the new channels. Of course, if the third wave termintes at exactly the original upper channel line first drawn from point N, the discarded channel and the new channel will be one and the same.

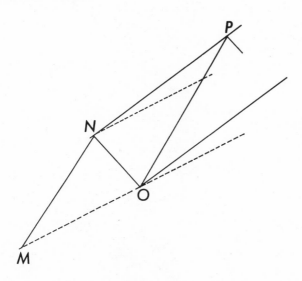

Figure 10

When wave four has terminated, either on, above, or below the new base line, the final channel can be drawn. This channel is quite important since its helps to locate the end of the fifth, or last, wave. It is on the termination of a long movement that investors and speculators must chiefly concentrate if their operations

---

[11] The extent of the inability to touch the upper channel line is irrelevant. Any such inability generally ushers in a severe reaction immediately.

are to prove successful. The final channel is located by drawing a connecting line between the extreme terminal or exposed contact of wave number two (O) and the terminal or exposed contact of wave number four (Q). Parallel to this base line, and touching the terminal of wave number three (P) is drawn another or upper channel line. This is shown in Figure 11, the discarded first and second channels of the diagram above having been erased for clarity of illustrations. Wave five should normally terminate at around the upper channel line, although this subject, because of its importance, will be treated in detail in the succeeding discussion outlining wave characteristics.

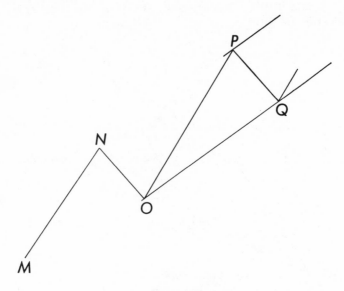

Figure 11

When the fifth wave has terminated, there will be a downward movement or correction of greater proportions than those previously recorded during the progress of the channel discussed above. This wave becomes number two of the next higher degree of movement, just as the first five waves previously channeled are now renumbered as wave number one of the next higher order. Channelling on a higher scale can be started at the termination of wave number two under the same principles as laid down above.

TERMINOLOGY

In classifying the wave movement as applied to the stock market (or as discerned in any other field of human activity, for that matter) it is necessary to devise some nomenclature by which the waves of any one degree will be distinguished from the waves of a greater or lower degree. For all practical purposes the following degrees of movement will cover such studies of the stock market as are herein presented, or as the student of market trends will need in his own research work in the phenomenon. The following order is from the lower to higher degrees, five waves of one degree going to make up the first wave of the next higher degree. Five Sub-Minuette waves, for example, compose wave number one of a Minuette movement, five Minuette waves equal wave number one of a Minute movement, and so on. The order follows:

Sub-Minuette
Minuette
Minute
Minor
Intermediate
Primary
Cycle
Super Cycle
Grand Super Cycle

To avoid confusion in the lettering of waves on charts presented herein, so that the movements of any one degree can be readily differentiated, at a glance, from the movements of another degree, the following number designations have been devised for the nine movements classified above.[12]

Degree	Number	Description
Sub-Minuette	a to e	Small letters
Minuette	A to E	Capitalized
Minute	1 to 5	Arabic Numerals
Minor	I to V	Roman Numerals
Intermediate	Ⓘ to Ⓥ	Romans circled
Primary	⓪Ⓘ to ⓪Ⓥ	Double circled
Cycle	c I to c V	Preceded by "c"
Super Cycle	sc I to sc V	Preceded by "sc"
Grand Super Cycle	gsc I to gsc V	Preceded by "gsc"

The reader need not pay too much attention, at the moment, to the above nomenclature and its numerical designation, but will find it of increasing usefulness as his studies into stock price movements progress.

A Grand Super Cycle in stock prices got under way in the United States in 1857[13]. The first wave of this degree of movement ran from 1857 to 1928. The second wave -- representing a correction of the first wave -- ran from November 1928 to 1932. The third wave[14] in the Grand Super Cycle started in 1932 and has many years to run.

The Grand Super Cycle wave from 1857 to 1928 is referred to as "No. 1", but it may have been No. 3 or No. 5. A severe depression occurred from 1854 to 1857 similar in duration to that of 1929-1932.

Wave number one[15] of the Grand Super Cycle, the upward wave that ran from 1857 to 1928, was made up of five waves which together may be designated as one complete Super Cycle. This Super Cycle may be subdivided as follows (see Figure 12):

1857-1864 -- Super Cycle Wave Number One
1864-1877 -- Super Cycle Correction (Wave Two)
1877-1881 -- Super Cycle Wave Number Three
1881-1896 -- Super Cycle Correction (Wave Four)
1896-1928 -- Super Cycle Wave Number Five

-----

12 Frost and I prefer a labeling system in which letters are reserved only for corrective waves while numbers are used for all impulse waves.

13 At the time of this book, Elliott's lack of data prior to 1857 resulted in an erroneous conclusion. 1857 marks the low of the second wave of the Grand Supercycle.

14 Actually the fifth. Frost and I break down the Grand Supercycle from 1789 in ELLIOTT WAVE PRINCIPLE -- KEY TO STOCK MARKET PROFITS. Elliott's use of 1857 as a Supercycle wave low is absolutely correct, but it is most definitely the end of the second and beginning of the third wave in the Grand Supercycle. While Elliott allows for this possibility in the next paragraph, he came firmly to this conclusion in the Interpretive Letter dated August 25, 1941 (see Figure 98 in Nature's Law).

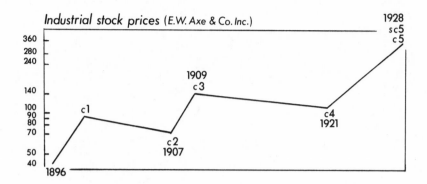

        The only record of stock prices available as far back as the beginning of the present Grand Super Cycle is the Axe-Houghton Index of representative issues (published in the New York Times Annalist) which records movements from 1854 to date.

        Let us, in further illustration, now take Super Cycle wave number five and break it down into its next smaller degree. This wave, running from 1896 to 1928, under the previously stated nomenclature, would be designated as a Cycle, and this Cycle would be made up of five waves. These waves were as follows (see Figure 13):[16]

1896-1899 -- Cycle Wave Number One
1899-1907 -- Cycle Correction (Wave Two)
1907-1909 -- Cycle Wave Number Three
1909-1921 -- Cycle Correction (Wave Four)
1921-1928 -- Cycle Wave Number Five

        If Cycle Wave Number Five -- the wave running from 1921 to 1928 -- be now reduced to its lesser degree,

---

[15] Three, actually.
[16] Frost and I prefer the count as presented in our book, although we use a different data series to arrive at our conclusions.

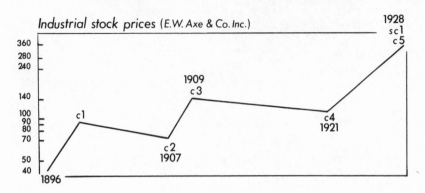

Figure 13

it will be found to have been composed of five Primary waves, as follows (see Figure 14):

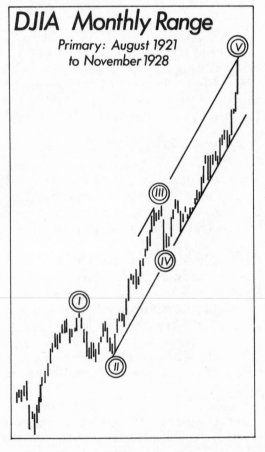

Figure 14

June 1921 to Mar. 1923 -- Primary Wave Number One
Mar. 1923 to May 1924 -- Primary Correction (Wave Two)
May 1924 to Nov. 1925 -- Primary Wave Number Three
Nov. 1925 to Mar. 1926 -- Primary Correction (Wave Four)
Mar. 1926 to Nov. 1928 -- Primary Wave Number Five

In like manner, the Primary waves of the Cyclical wave running from June 1921 to November 1928 can each be broken down into Intermediate waves; the Intermediate waves can each be broken down into Minor waves; and so on through lesser and lesser degree until the most minute movement of record is properly analyzed and classified.

November 28, 1928, with the Dow Jones average of thirty industrial stocks standing at 295.62, came at the end of the fifth Minuette wave of the fifth Minute wave of the fifth Minor wave of the fifth Intermediate wave of the fifth Primary wave of the fifth Cycle wave of the fifth Super Cycle wave of the first Grand Super Cycle wave. Stated otherwise, one who was tracing the stock market's pattern in terms of its decade by decade, year by year, month by month, week by week, day by day, and hour by hour fluctuations, was not confused as to its trend during any part of the past decade but was able, even, to fix not only the year and month when the great bull market terminated, but could even determine the day and hour of the end -- and even the minute. From the Super Cycle down through every lesser degree to the most infinitesimal movement recorded, the market, before reaching its final peak, had to complete a fifth wave of each lesser degree.

It will have been noted that the top of the fifth wave of the Super Cycle is shown as having ended November 1928 (the orthodox top) and not September 1929, the extreme high.[17] Between these points are registered (see Figure 15):

-- Wave "A" November to December 1928 (down) and
-- Wave "B" December 1928 to September 1929 (up in three minor waves), in an irregular reversal.

-----

[17] Frost and I allow for other interpretations as well, particularly that 1929 marked the orthodox top.

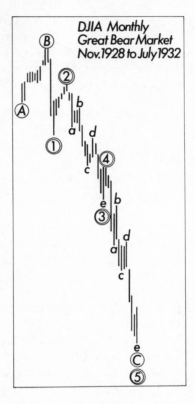

Figure 15

-- Wave "C" runs from September 1929 to July 1932. "C" was subdivided into five waves down, and the irregular top signalled a fast straight down movement. The first reversal downward in December 1928 was signalled by the extended fifth wave (minor) up to November 1928.

The same irregular pattern occurred at the top of August 1937.[18] This irregular pattern is described in detail under the caption "Corrections."

---

[18] Questionable. See footnote #42.

WAVE CHARACTERISTICS

In the preceding discussions an attempt has been made to state, as simply as possible, the five-wave phenomenon. In the present discussion attention will be devoted more to detail, in order that the student of the wave movement can fully master the subject, and thus be prepared to develop his own studies of price and other movements of human origin and influence.

Investors and speculators in stocks are particularly concerned with the termination point of a fifth wave as this event marks the point at which an entire movement is to be corrected by a reverse movement of similar degree. Stock market movements of important dimensions, such as Intermediate swings running over a number of months, and Primary swings running over a number of years, will witness, at termination, a considerable price correction, and such terminal points call for disposition of stock holdings. It is likewise important that terminal corrections be identified, as these points represent price areas where long positions in stocks are to be established. In the following paragraphs the fifth wave, as well as the corrective wave, are dwelt upon rather fully. Other factors bearing on terminal points are also discussed.

The Fifth Wave

In fixing the end of a movement in stock prices, it should be borne in mind that before the movement has terminated there must be five waves of the next lesser degree of movement; that the fifth wave of such next lesser degree will also require five waves of a still next lesser degree, and so on. For illustration, an Intermediate movement will end on the fifth Sub-Minuette wave of the fifth Minuette wave of the fifth Minute wave of the fifth Minor wave of such Intermediate movement. In Figure 16, the fifth Minor wave has been broken down into its five Minuette waves, and the fifth Minuette wave has been broken down into its five Sub-Minuette waves to illustrate the foregoing principle.[19]

The fifth wave of a movement, particularly the

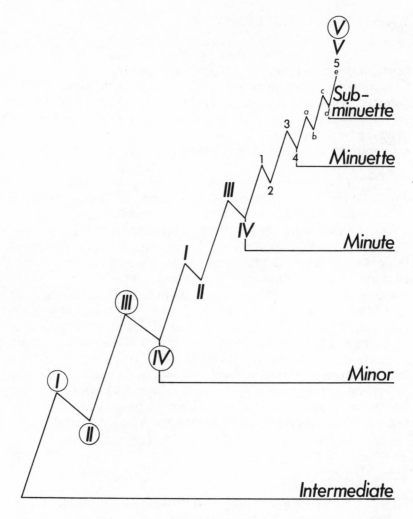

Figure 16

larger such as the Intermediate, and above, generally penetrates or "throws over" the upper parallel line formed by channelling the termination points of the second, third and fourth waves as described in the preceding discussion, and as illustrated in Figure 17.

---

19 Elliott adopted a loose form of illustration in order to make more economical use of vertical space in his books. I have changed proportions occasionally to adhere to normal wave characteristics. Exceptions are the figures in the Financial World articles, which I left intact as Elliott had them.

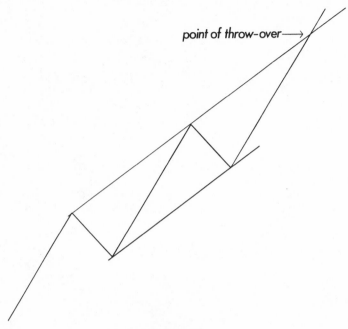

point of throw-over⟶

Figure 17

Volume tends to climb on a throw-over, and when this throw-over is by the fifth Intermediate wave of a Primary movement, volume should be very heavy. When the fifth wave of any degree fails to penetrate or throw over its upper channel line and decline occurs, this is a warning of weakness. The extent of the weakness indicated is according to the degree of the wave.

Sometimes, at near a point of throw-over, a fifth wave will fail to immediately complete and the fourth wave flattens out before number five starts (see Figure 18).

In locating "throw-overs," a logarithmic scale is highly recommended for those charts on which the market or individual stocks may be followed by means of the weekly price range, whereas an arithmetic scale should be used for daily range and hourly charts. At the tops of primary and higher degree movements the arithmetic scale is much more likely to produce throw-overs, whereas at the bottom of such movements the reverse is true, that is, the logarithmic scale is more apt to develop throw-overs. In both cases the arithmetic scale would be

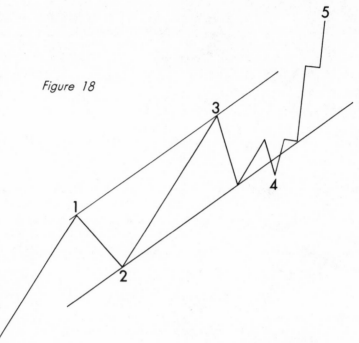

Figure 18

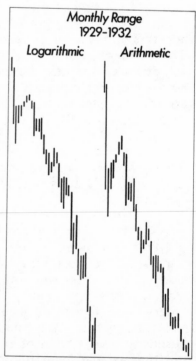

deceptive in waves of say 30 points or more. To clearly illustrate one of the foregoing statements, a monthly range chart of the 1929-1932 movement of the Dow Jones Industrial Average on both the logarithmic and the arithmetic scales is shown in Figure 19.

Fifth waves will sometimes deploy or spread out. This has been designated as one type of "stretching." In such an event the fifth wave, rather than the terminating movement of which it was a part, is followed by four other waves of lower degree. That is, the fifth wave has

Monthly Range
1929-1932

Logarithmic　　Arithmetic

Figure 19

simply subdivided into five waves. Stretching is a characteristic of markets that are unusually strong (or weak, where the stretching occurs in a down movement). Examples of upside stretching were witnessed in the 1921-1928 upswing, the culmination of a seventy-two year advance.

Corrections

While the Wave Principle is very simple and exceedingly useful in forecasting, nevertheless there are refinements within the Principle that may baffle the student, especially when wave movements are in process of formation. The best way to explain what is meant by refinements is to chart them. The examples are theoretically perfect specimens; the student will find the actual development of these patterns not so simple in all cases.[20]

Corrections always have 3 waves[21] and fall into four general types, but while in formation it is sometimes difficult to forecast the exact pattern and extent.[20]   Once completed, the pattern indicates the

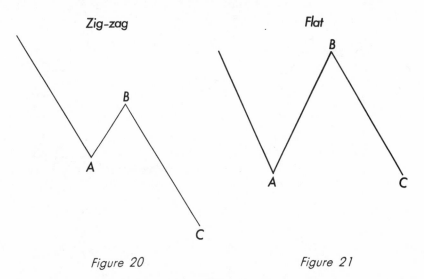

Zig-zag

Flat

Figure 20   *Figure 21*

---

[20] This type of comment surely helps moderate charges of Elliott's absolutism and dogmatism.
[21] Unless they are triangles. Later Elliott discovered double threes and triple threes. These variations, along with double zigzags, were later added in Nature's Law.

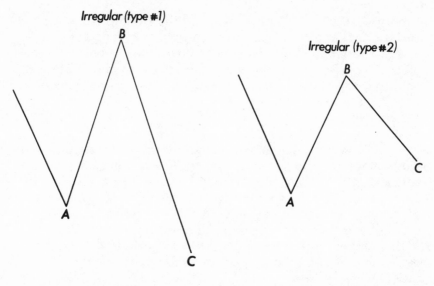

Figure 22   Figure 23

strength of the ensuing move. The types shown in Figures 20 through 23 are those of very small corrections. The general outlines of patterns are the same in all degrees. The same types as above, but for larger degrees, are shown in Figures 24 through 26.

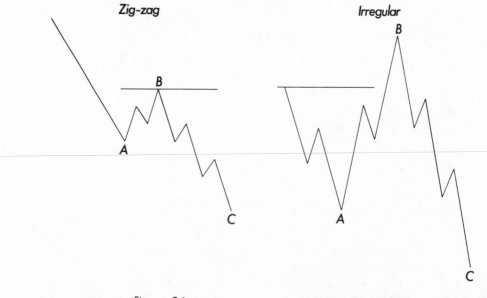

Figure 24   Figure 25

Flat

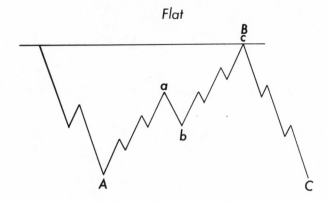

Figure 26

Still larger types of corrections, although of the same general patterns, are those seen in Intermediate and Primary degrees (see Figures 27 through 29).

Zig-zag

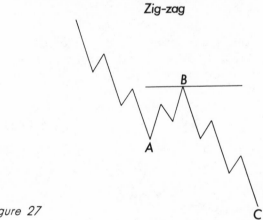

Figure 27

Flat

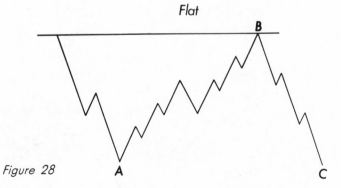

Figure 28

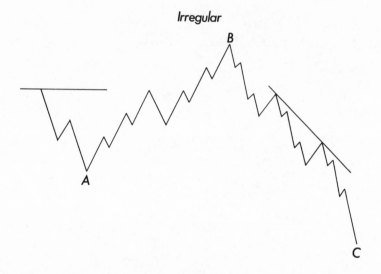

Irregular

Figure 29

Extensions

Extensions may appear in any one of the three impulses, waves Nos. 1, 3 or 5, but rarely in more than one. Usually they occur in No. 5.[22] Examples are shown in Figure 30.

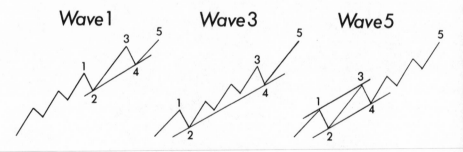

Figure 30

---

[22] Despite Elliott's contention, experience shows that wave three is most often the extended wave. Elliott's experience with the 1921-1929 and 1932-1937 bull markets, both of which contained extended fifth waves, surely influenced his thinking on this point.

Extensions of Extensions

The same rules govern both extensions and extensions of extensions. In Figure 31 will be found three types of extensions of extensions and the standard type.

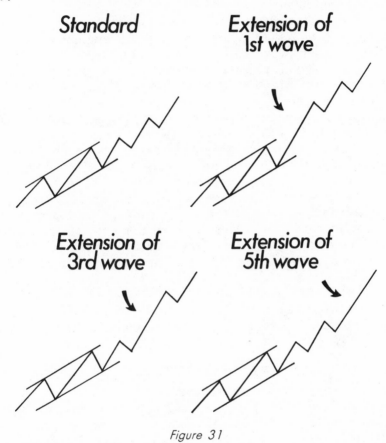

Figure 31

Behavior of Market Following Extensions

A thorough understanding of extensions is very important. Warnings of this phenomenon have been sought without success and for certain reasons it is probable none exist.[23] However, losses can be avoided

---

[23] Absolutely true, as far as I can tell. There are some guidelines, as Frost and I point out in our book, but no rules. See Footnote #11 in the Financial World articles and the corresponding text.

and profits obtained by learning the behavior of the market subsequent to their occurrence. The rules are:

1) Extensions occur in new territory of the current cycle, and
2) Are retraced twice.[24]
3) The first retracement will occur immediately in three waves to approximately the beginning of the extension (wave 2 of the extension).
4) The second retracement will occur in the usual progress of the market and travel beyond the extension.
5) However, when an extension occurs, for example, at the end of a fifth primary (where a major reversal is due) the first and second retracements become waves A and B of an irregular correction. This complies with the double retracement rules. Wave C will be composed of five waves downward, fast and probably to the beginning of the fifth primary of the preceding bull market.[25] The only example[26] of this particular kind is downward from November 1928, upward to September 1929 and downward to 1932. (See Figure 15.)

6) Occasionally extensions occur in bear markets under the same rules, such as, for example, during October 1937.

---

[24] Extensions are retraced twice only if the extension occurs in the fifth impulse wave.

[25] Usually, although not necessarily. An irregular correction will sometimes hold above the beginning of the fifth primary of the preceding bull market. See ELLIOTT WAVE PRINCIPLE -- KEY TO STOCK MARKET PROFITS.

[26] This example is not a particularly good one. The extension in the fifth wave of the 1921-1928 rise was not retraced the first time (that is, to the "beginning of the extension") by wave A as Elliott counts it, since wave A was extremely short. Wave C as Elliott counts it did retrace much of the fifth wave twice, once in the October 1929 crash and again in the 1930 rally. A different count, one which labels the bottom of the October 1929 crash as "A" (an irregular a-b-c from the 1928 orthodox top) and the 1930 rally as "B," (an inverted zigzag) would better satisfy the double retracement rule.

7)   An extension is never the end of a movement.[27]
     This does not infer that higher or lower levels may
     not be seen even without an extension.

8)   Retracement means that the travel of a described
     movement between two specified points is covered
     again. For example, a correction and resumption of
     the trend is a double retracement.

        If a trader is holding "longs" when a downward
extension appears, he should not sell then because the
market will immediately retrace the extension in three
waves[28] before seeking lower levels.

        Important extensions have occurred as follows:

Industrials Upward   Industrials Downward
July-November 1925   November 1929
October-November 1928   October 1937
July 1933
March 1936   Rails Upward
                            February 1936

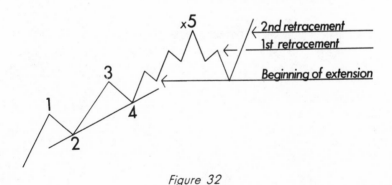

Figure 32

---

[27] The orthodox end of a "movement" in the direction
of the main trend is the terminal point of the fifth wave
of a five-wave sequence. What Elliott appears to be
saying here is that when an extension occurs in the fifth
wave up, an irregular top will carry the market into new
high ground, thereby extending the "movement" beyond
the orthodox top of the fifth wave.
[28] Again, only if it occurs in a fifth wave down.

While the first retracement will occur immediately and in three waves, the second might not develop for a considerable time but it will eventually and in the current cycle. The pattern of an extension[29] and double retracement is illustrated in Figure 32.

An irregular top above an extension

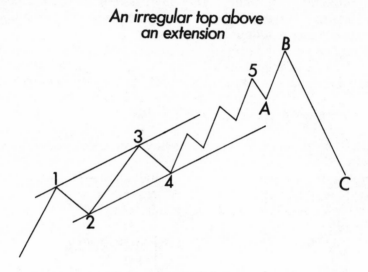

Figure 33

An irregular top above an ordinary advance

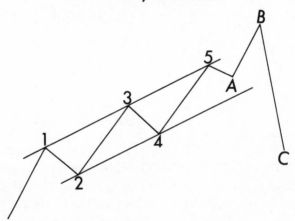

Figure 34

[29] Elliott's use of "x5" to notate an extended wave is very useful. Few students have employed it.

Irregular Corrections

Examples of corrections have already been shown, but not as a part of the waves of the previous movement being corrected. Such examples are shown in Figures 33 and 34. The letters A, B and C indicate waves one, two and three of the corrective movement, irregular pattern. Note that the second wave, B, exceeds the orthodox top (5) of the previous movement.

Strong Corrections

Corrections can prove useful as warnings of strong movements. Figure 35 is a regular zig-zag pattern, which indicates ordinary strength of subsequent movement. Figure 36 is a flat, indicating strong subsequent movement (see No. 4 Primary, July 1933 to July 1934).

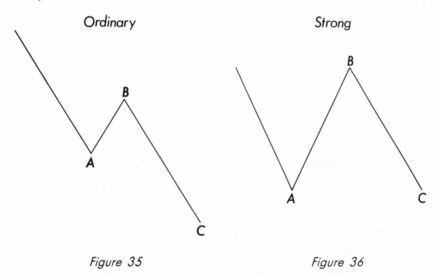

Ordinary

Strong

Figure 35

Figure 36

Figure 37 shows a pattern where the end of the correction at "2" is higher than the end of wave A of the correction, indicating unusual strength of the subsequent movement. (The second correction shown in Figure 37 is weaker.)

Corrections of bear trends, that is, corrections following downward movements, have the same characteristics as those of advancing movements, but in reverse (see Figures 38 through 40).

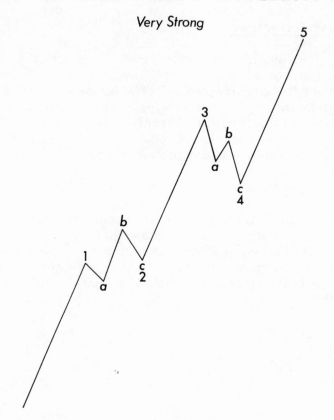

Figure 37

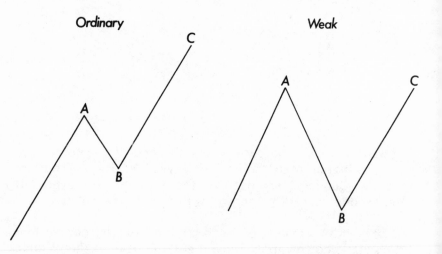

Figure 38 *Figure 39*

Very Weak

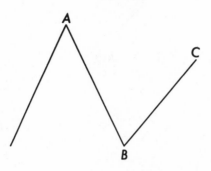

Figure 40

    Irregular corrections in bear trends are also seen, but very rarely. Note that after a five wave downtrend, an irregular correction would appear as in Figure 41.

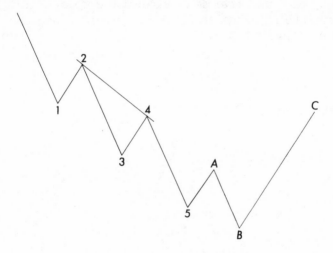

Figure 41

Failures

    In the pattern shown in Figure 42, the fifth wave failed to materialize and stock should be sold at "B." Note that there are five waves down from the top at "3," whereas a correction should be composed of three waves. The answer is that "B" is the real top from which only three waves downward were registered. That is, the decline stole two waves from the advance. Put in another

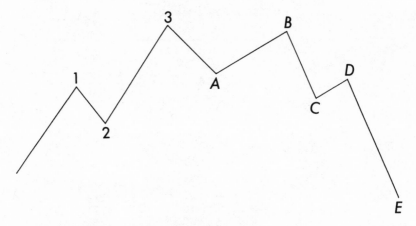

Figure 42

way, the regular number upward is five plus the regular number down is three, total eight. In this case there were three upward and five downward, same total eight. Such patterns are rare but are a serious warning and should be acted upon immediately.

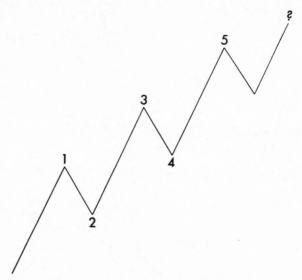

Figure 43

When the Student Is In Doubt

In the position shown in Figure 43, the trader may not know which of the following patterns will develop, i.e., an extension or an irregular correction. Volume may furnish the answer. Elsewhere it is stated that volume diminishes during the various waves of correction (zig-zags, flats, triangles), therefore if volume is extremely light in the last wave shown, then it is wave B of an irregular correction. If relatively heavy, an extension is generating.[30]

Triangles

        Wave movements occasionally taper off to a point or broaden out from a point in the form of a triangle. These triangular formations are important since they indicate the direction the market will take at the conclusion or approximate apex of the triangle.

        Triangles are of two classes -- horizontal and diagonal. Horizontal triangles represent hesitation on the part of prices. At the conclusion of a horizontal triangle the market will resume the same trend -- upward or downward -- which it was pursuing previous to triangular hesitation. Horizontal triangles are simply hesitations and have the same significance as flats. If a zigzag appears at No. 2, a flat or triangle will appear at No. 4 (see Figure 44).[31] If a flat or triangle occurs at No. 2, a zigzag will appear at No. 4 (see Figure 45).[32]

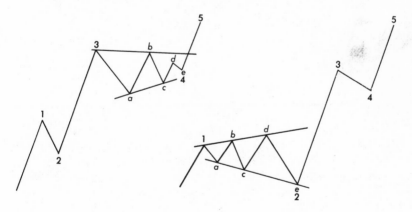

Figure 44   Figure 45

Examples of horizontal triangles are shown in Figure 46. They are of four types.

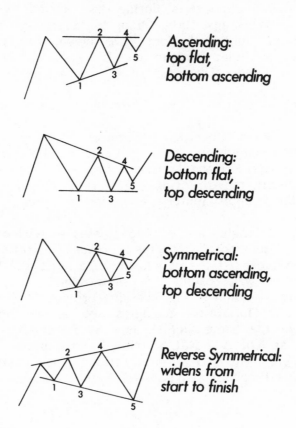

Ascending:
top flat,
bottom ascending

Descending:
bottom flat,
top descending

Symmetrical:
bottom ascending,
top descending

Reverse Symmetrical:
widens from
start to finish

Figure 46

---

[30] This statement is true for small degrees, but not true for waves of higher than Intermediate degree. The 1961-62 rally occurred on extremely high volume and was a "B" wave. The 1930 rally, a corrective wave advance, occurred on volume higher than that at the peak in 1929.

[31] This rule is part of what was later dubbed the Rule of Alternation.

[32] Elliott later modified his rules to indicate that a triangle always precedes the final impulse wave in a sequence. Thus a triangle can never occur as wave two in a five-wave sequence, only as wave four (or as wave B in an A-B-C correction).

Examples of diagonal triangles are shown in Figure 47. They are of two types.

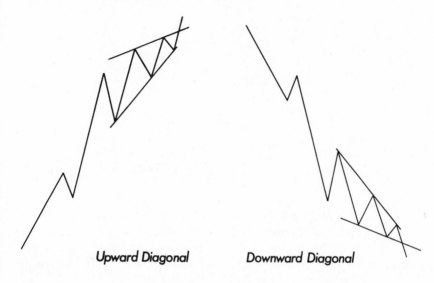

Upward Diagonal   Downward Diagonal

Figure 47

Triangles, whether horizontal or diagonal, as will be noted from the above illustration, contain five waves. Where there are less than five waves, the triangle falls outside the wave phenomenon, as herein discussed, and should be ignored.

The most important thing to be noted with respect to a horizontal triangle is where it begins. This is because wave number two of the triangle must be definitely fixed, and to fix wave number two it becomes necessary to identify wave number one. Wave number two is important, because when the triangle has ended the market will move from the triangle in the same direction as wave two travelled.[33] In Figure 48, the direction of wave two of the horizontal triangle is downward. At the conclusion of the fifth triangular wave, the market, which has been hesitating during the course of its downward travel M-N, will resume the decline.

In Figure 49, the record of the five triangular

---

[33] This discussion is superfluous if one understands the wave position of the formations.

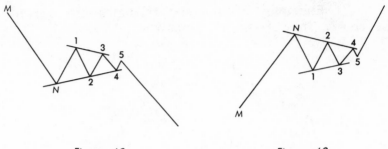

Figure 48   Figure 49

waves is upward. The market bottomed at M and is hesitating after the upward movement M-N, prior to resuming the advance.

In Figure 50, wave two of the upward diagonal triangle is downward. The market will reverse its direction at the end of this diagonal (that is, when the fifth triangular wave has terminated) and will return to about the base of the triangle, as illustrated.

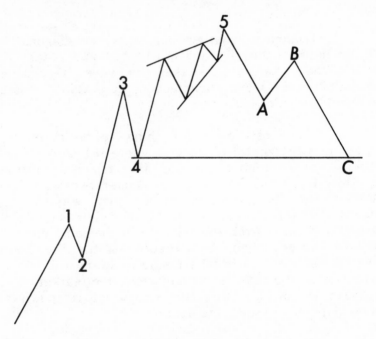

Figure 50

The fifth wave of all but reverse triangles frequently falls short of its channel or triangle line. Occasionally, however, as shown in the illustration above, fifth wave will penetrate its triangle line.

If the last wave (the fifth Intermediate) of a Primary movement develops a triangle,[34] be prepared for a rapid reversal.

All waves in a triangle must be part of a movement in one direction. Otherwise no triangle is present, only a coincidence.

A diagonal triangle occurs only as a fifth wave, that is, it should have four waves back of it of the same degree as it will be.

When the range (weekly or daily) in a triangle embraces the entire width of the triangle, the end has about arrived. Confirmation should be required in wave number five. A throw-over is not essential.

Usually triangles are quite small and all waves are not developed in detail. For the first time, between October 1937 and February 1938, one occurred of sufficiently large proportions to demonstrate that all five waves should be composed of three minors. Each of these five waves formed a different pattern.[35]

The Dow Jones Industrial Average does not show this period as a triangle, but the Standard Statistics, 348 stocks, weekly range, makes a perfect picture as shown in Figure 51, a perfect triangle and the largest on record. Being a weekly range, it does not show the composition of each of the five waves, but another average daily range displays them as shown in Figure 66, Chapter IX.

---

[34] That is, a diagonal triangle.
[35] A very important point. This is another facet of the Rule of Alternation.

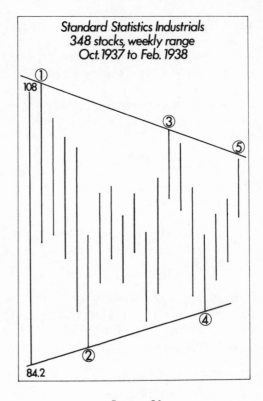

Figure 51

SPEED, VOLUME AND CHARTING[36]

      High speed by the market in one direction almost invariably produces a corresponding high speed in the reversal, as for example, the midsummer 1932 advance covered forty points (Dow Jones Industrial Average) or 100% in nine weeks. This was equal to 4 1/2 points per week. Note the decreasing speed of advances from 1932 to 1937 in Figure 52.

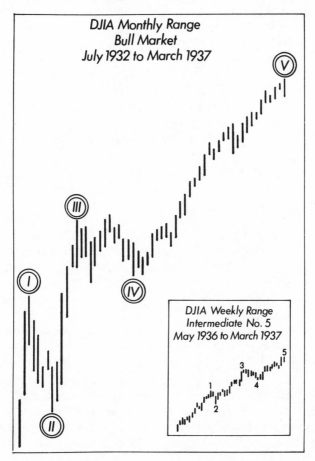

Figure 52

---

[36] Based on the abrupt changes in organizational style (and other small points, such as spelling), I conclude that Chapters VI, VII and IX undoubtedly were written by Elliott and inserted by him after Collins' manuscript was completed.

In fast markets like the advance of 1932 and 1933, it is essential to observe the daily as well as the weekly ranges, otherwise characteristics of importance may be hidden, such as, for example, triangles and extensions.

In a subsequent heading entitled "Charting," a reference is made to "lines." In the average market, slow speed and the exclusive use of daily range may conceal important patterns. Take, for example, the period from the last week of January to the first week in June, 1904, five months during which the maximum range of daily closings (Dow Jones Industrial Average) was only 4.09 points (50.50 - 46.41). On the daily chart the appearance is an uninteresting line, but when condensed into a weekly range chart a perfect triangle is disclosed, with the second wave pointing upward, thus assuring the trader that the market would move upward following the end of the triangle.

Volume

Volume decreases gradually from the beginning to the end of horizontal triangles, flats and other types of corrections. Volume often helps to clarify the character of a movement. However, when markets are abnormally "thin," the usual volume signals are sometimes deceptive.

Characteristics of volume are very impressive when considered in conjunction with the five-wave cycle. For example, during an advance or a decline of some importance, volume will increase during number one wave, diminish during number two, increase during number three, decrease during number four, and increase during number five. Immediately following number five, volume should be fairly well maintained, with little, if any, further progress in price, indicating reversal.

Herein reference is made to volume and ratio. "Volume" is the actual number of shares transferred, whereas "ratio" is the ratio of volume to listed shares on the New York Stock Exchange.

In its bulletin for July 1938, the New York

Stock Exchange noted in chart form some interesting comparisons of volume and ratio. An upward ratio cycle started in 1914 and completed five primaries, ending in 1929. Then began a downward cycle, ending June 18, 1938 (see Figure 53).

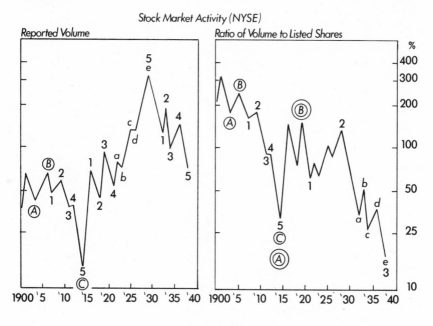

Figure 53

Precisely the same phenomenon occurred in the price of seats on the New York Stock Exchange (see Figures 54 and 55).

The ratio waves are not easy to follow in minor detail for the reason that volume varies according to the momentary direction of the market. However, as fluctuations in stock exchange seats are not affected by the momentary direction of the market, these become a useful guide to the ratio scale. See chapter X, "The Wave Principle in Other Fields."

According to the bulletins of the New York Stock Exchange, page 11, the ratio for May 1928 was 12.48%, and the ratio for May 1938 was 0.98%. I calculate that the ratio for the first 18 days of June 1938 was 0.65%. On Saturday, June 18, 1938, actual volume

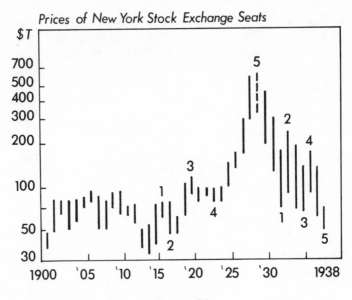

Figure 54

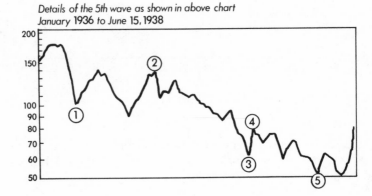

Figure 55

was 104,000 shares, equivalent to say 200,000 shares for a five-hour session. For several weeks previous to June 18 volume was so low that long intervals frequently occurred between sales of important stocks in the averages, with the result that occasionally Sub-Minuette waves failed to appear in the hourly waves, or registered when they should not. Hourly volume was occasionally deceptive for the same reason. Fortunately such low volume should not recur for some twenty years.

On the first page of its monthly bulletin for November 1937, the New York Stock Exchange noted volume ratio to price change of the period between August 14 and October 1937 and seven other periods of equal duration. I have reduced the comparison to percentage and find that the 1937 period was by far the most remarkable of all.

The following outline of comparisons is interesting:

Recent bear market
Top, March 10, 1937,   195.59
Bottom, March 31, 1938,   97.46
Decline,   98.13 points,
                                        or 50.1%.

Time: 1 year, 3 weeks.

Money value of stock transactions on the N.Y.S.E.
March, 1937, $2,612,000,000
May, 1938,   499,000,000
June, 1938 (est.)   187,000,000
Decline: 92.9%.

Time: 1 year, 4 months.

Price-Volume Ratio for 64-Day Periods (which was the duration of decline from August 14 to October 19, 1937. Comparisons of this with other periods is as follows):

August 14 - October 19, 1937, 22.2%.
March-May 1937, 10.9%.
Late 1929, 11.1%.
February-April 1934, 6.5%.
Other periods, 2.1% to 1.0%.

New York Stock Exchange Seats
Top, 1929: $625,000
Bottom, June 15, 1938:   51,000
Decline: 92%.

Time: 9 years.

Volume decline from March 1937 to June 1938 was 87.5%.

Data obtained from the Public Relations Department relative to money value of transactions are shown in Figure 56.

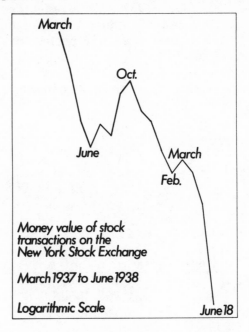

Figure 56

MISCELLANEOUS NOTES: CHARTING

1) Tops of big moves scatter or fan out in different groups and stocks, whereas bottoms of big moves consolidate; that is, different groups and stocks tend to establish lows simultaneously. During July 1932, for instance, bonds, stocks, production, insurance sales, and many other major spheres of human activity bottomed together (see Figures 69 through 79, Chapter X). That, of course, was a bottom to number two[37] wave of the Grand Supercycle and therefore the phenomenon was naturally drastically emphasized.

2) When, in the course of a move, the numbering becomes confused, the relative size of waves may help to distinguish one degree of movement from another. The use of the exposed contacts (that is, channeling them) should help to clarify the movement.

3) Always connect or channel two exposed contacts.

4) Always await development of point number four and the drawing of the final channel before determining culmination of the move (that is, the approximate point where wave five should end).

5) Width of channels must be preserved in all movements of the same category, or, stated in other words, the width of a channel of the same movement must be preserved,[38] except that number five may not reach the top of the channel.

6) The larger the category, the more probability of a throw-over.

7) In channeling: on an advance, the base line is below; on a decline, above.

8) Strength for the main move is indicated when the base line is hugged. See the movement from January 1927 to June 1928 in Figure 14 as one illustration.

---

[37] Four, actually.
[38] I.e., "Keep the channel lines parallel."

9) In order to properly visualize the wave phenomenon in its larger aspects, certain methods of charting are
essential, as follows:

-- Weekly range of the daily extreme high and low, on
logarithmic scale, preferably exaggerated two or three
times the usual practice.

-- One sheet for each complete advance of five
primaries, and its correction.

10) These recommendations apply to the three
principal averages (Industrial, Rail, Utility), to small
groups and individual stocks. The daily range of the three
averages, of groups and of individual stocks in which the
investor may be interested, should also be maintained, and
ordinary arithmetic scale is satisfactory.

11) There are three important reasons why weekly
range charts are necessary:

-- Only by this method is it possible to observe the
movement over a sufficient historical background in order
to judge the nature of the several degrees of waves,
especially the larger.

-- So-called "lines" are converted into patterns of flats or
triangles, composed of three or five waves respectively
(useful in determining or confirming future
movements).[39]

-- Any deceptions of the small daily range are obviated.

12) Always place the particular movement under
supervision, whether it be a Minute, Minor, Intermediate,
Primary or even greater degree, on one chart. Otherwise
the numbering of waves, their relative magnitude, and the
channeling of movements become distorted and confused.

13) The best time measures for Primary and lesser

---

[39] In my experience, the daily movement always seems
to clarify the structure of the weekly, not the other way
around. A structure visible on weekly charts must break
down correctly on the daily and hourly if one's conclusions
are to be valid.

movements are weekly, daily and hourly charts. Never be guided entirely by any one of these three important time measures, but keep them all in mind in analyzing wave numbers. In fast markets the hourly and daily movements are the best guides; in slow markets, the daily and weekly.

14) For the first time since 1928, stocks, bonds and volume ratio got into gear June 18, 1938. Only with a knowledge of the Wave Principle may these phenomena be observed and followed.

15) Some items appear to have declined in five waves. In such cases an "irregular" top occurred and wave "C" thereof was composed of five waves, as explained under the title "Corrections."

16) In some cases it is impossible to obtain figures for charting, such as Real Estate, for the reason that there is no central market, the items are not standardized, and prices specified in transfers are often "nominal." The solution is found in "foreclosed mortgages." Reliable figures of these are available. When foreclosures are at a bottom, Real Estate is at a top, and vice versa.

17) In other cases, while reliable figures are available, it is difficult to define the minor degrees. An example is volume which fluctuates in minor degree with the momentary direction of the market. The solution is found in prices of New York Stock Exchange seats.[40]

18) Seasonal fluctuations present difficulties which may be overcome by charting a ten year average of weeks, months or quarters, using same as a ratio basis. For example, weekly statistics of car loadings are available and the ratio of the current week to the ten year average may be charted, thus disclosing the facts needed on which to base an interpretation under the Wave Principle.

---

[40] This rather cryptic assertion is better stated in Chapter VI. Even so, since seat prices are not actively traded enough to register in minor degree, it is difficult to see how their waves could help clarify the minor degree.

19) When two items which do not always travel in harmony unite occasionally, unusual disturbance may take place, such as that described under the title "Volume."

20) Not all stocks perform harmoniously. While the principal averages topped on March 10, 1937, the several Standard Statistics groups commenced to top in Novemeber 1936, increased to the maximum number in March, then gradually decreased until May. On the other hand, stocks tend to bottom simultaneously.

APPLYING THE WAVE PRINCIPLE

As stated in a previous chapter, the investor and speculator are greatly concerned with the termination of a fifth wave, for this marks the point at which an entire movement is to be corrected by a reversal. Stock market moves of high degree, particularly intermediate movements running over a number of months, and primary movements running over a number of years will witness, at termination, considerable price correction, and the terminal points thus call for disposition of long positions. It is likewise important that terminal points of corrections be identified, as there are price areas where long positions can most profitably be re-established.

A first consideration of an operator in stocks is to determine over what type of movement he wishes to carry a long position in stocks. Many investors prefer to operate through a Primary movement and it is this type of movement which will be discussed here, although the same principles that apply to this movement will likewise apply to a movement of lesser degree or greater degree.

Let us assume that the investor has correctly established a long position in June 1921. From his study of the Grand Super Cycle (see Figure 12) he sees that the market started as a Super Cycle movement in 1857 and that Cycle movements one, two, three and four of the entire Super Cycle movement have been completed. The fifth Cycle movement started in 1896 and is nearly completed, in that four Primary waves have elapsed from 1896 to 1921. Primary movement number five is just commencing. It will be made up of five Intermediate movements. Intermediate movement number five will not only terminate the full Primary movement, but it will also terminate a full Cycle and a full Super Cycle. The period ahead, in other words, promises to be quite interesting.

Based upon his study of Primary movements one and three preceding the fifth one now getting under way, the investor has some gauge as to the extent and length of the movement, although, as previously mentioned, these are but rough guides due to modifying events which serve to differentiate one wave of a certain degree from another wave of the same degree. A more certain guide, however, can be derived from channelling. The Super Cycle running from 1857 has completed four waves of lesser degree (Cycle movements) and thus by connecting exposed contacts of wave terminals two and four of the Super Cycle and drawing a parallel line across the terminal point of wave three, an upper parallel is established, about which line the fifth Cycle, or that running from 1896, should end, thus completing wave five of the Super Cycle movement. Similarly, the Cycle movement from 1896 has completed four waves (Primary movements) so that, as for the Super Cycle, it can be given its final upper channel line about which the fifth Primary movement now under way should terminate.

At this point the investor, whose set purpose is to hold stocks purchased in June 1921 until the primary movement then starting has terminated, observes those rules which will help him in selling out. Some of these rules have been previously stated; others are first presented at this time.

1) The Primary movement will be made up of five Intermediate waves. Selling is not to be considered until four Intermediate waves have been witnessed, and the fifth is under way.

2) When the fourth Intermediate wave has terminated, and the fifth gets under way, it will be composed of five lesser degree or Minor waves, and selling is not to be considered until the fifth Minor wave is under way.

3) When the fourth Minor wave of the fifth Intermediate wave has terminated, and the fifth Minor wave gets under way, it will not terminate until five Minute waves have been witnessed and selling is not to be considered ahead of the fifth Minute wave.

4) It is probable that the fifth Minute wave of the fifth Minor wave of the fifth Intermediate wave will also be made up, based upon hourly averages, of five Minuette waves, the fifth of which waves will likewise be composed of five Sub-Minuette waves. To reach the extreme top of the Primary wave starting in June 1921, therefore, it will not be necessary to liquidate holdings until the fifth Sub-Minuette wave of the fifth Minuette wave of the

fifth Minute wave of the fifth Minor wave of the fifth Intermediate wave has terminated.

5) The fifth wave of a Super Cycle movement, of a Cycle movement and of a Primary movement generally penetrate or "throw over" the upper channel line established for the termination limit of each such movement. Upper channel lines (see earlier paragraphs) have been established for the termination limit of the fifth Super Cycle wave and the fifth Cycle wave. Since the Primary movement starting in June 1921 will end a Cycle as well as a Super Cycle movement (see Figure 13), it may be anticipated that such Primary movement will not have ended until it has carried prices (on a logarithmic scale) above the upper channel lines of the Super Cycle and the Cycle. Likewise, the fifth Intermediate movement of the existing Primary -- an Intermediate movement that is yet ahead -- should penetrate or throw over the upper channel line established for it.

6) Terminal points of the fifth wave of Super Cycle, Cycle, and Primary movements are usually accompanied by heavy volume of trading relative to prior waves of each such movement. Intense volume should therefore be witnessed during and near the peak of the fifth Intermediate wave of the Primary movement now getting under way.

With the above general rules in mind, the investor lets the market unfold, plotting its weekly and monthly movement in order to keep abreast of each Intermediate move as it occurs. The weekly movement is given in Figures 57 through 61. Intermediate movement number one terminates in March 1923. It is made up of five Minor swings, as a glance at Figure 57 will indicate. There follows Intermediate movement number two made up, as should be the case for even numbered or corrective movements, of three movements. Intermediate movement number three runs to November 1925. It is succeeded by the usual three wave correction.[41]

----

[41] This discussion terminates abruptly and leads me to believe that a page was omitted from the monograph as published. In any case, the later paragraphs of Chapter IV can serve to complete the discussion.

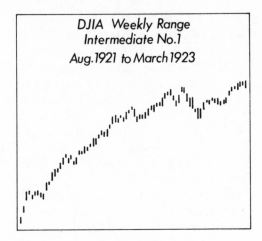

Figure 57

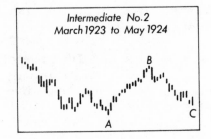

Figure 58

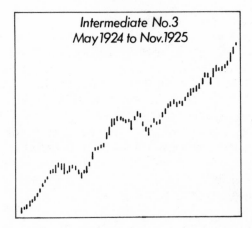

Figure 59

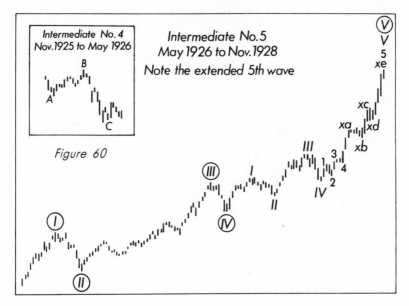

Figure 61

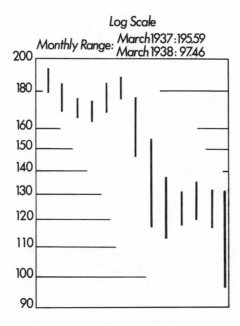

Figure 62

RARITIES IN THE 1937–1938 BEAR MARKET

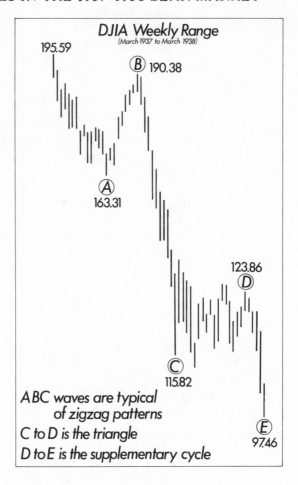

Figure 63

The 1937–1938 bear market (see Figures 62 and 63) provided a number of novelties, for example:

Parallelogram

August 4, 1937, at 187.31, was the "orthodox" top of a rally.[42] then followed a dip of three waves and an advance of three waves to 190.38, August 14. Between these two dates waves A and B of an irregular correction were formed (see Figure 65). Wave C was very rapid and long, down to 115.82 on October 18, and formed a perfect parallelogram. It has no particular significance for

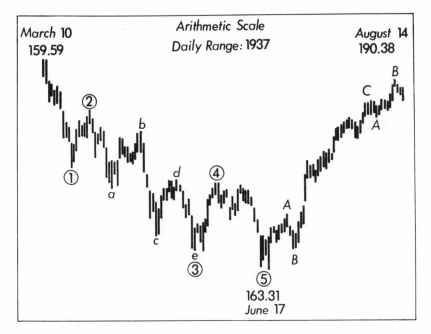

Figure 64

that reason. The speed and extent were spectacular, and indicated by the "irregular" top, the same as that of 1928-1929-1932 (see Figure 65).

42 Elliott should have interpreted this juncture differently based on typical wave structure and "look." The supposed waves A and B are way out of proportion to the huge C. Wave C as he labels it is actually wave three of the five-wave decline which constitutes wave A of the 1937-1942 A-B-C bear market. Therefore the orthodox top of wave two is August 14 at 190.38 and is followed by five waves down for wave three, as it should be. A correct count for Figure 64 would be as follows: Where Elliott has a circled 1, place a 1; where he has small b, place a 2, completing an irregular correction (which, by the way, subdivides perfectly); where he has small c, place a 3; where he has small d, place a 4; where he has a circled 3, place a 5. Then an irregular correction upward follows: where he has a circled 4, place an A; where he has a circled 5, place a B; then a C can be placed at the August 14 high on the top of a clear nine-wave advance (five waves with an extension).

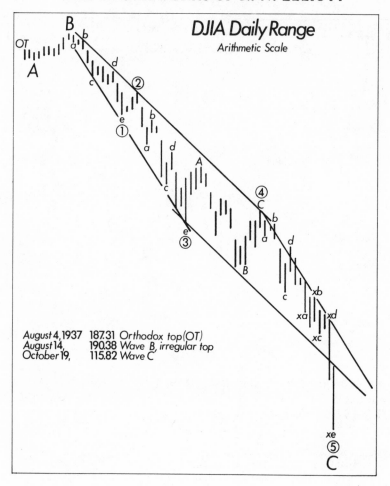

Figure 65

Figure 65 embodies the greatest number of interesting features known to the author. Note the parallelogram pattern. The "irregular" top, OT to B, forecasts a severe decline. The extension xa to xe forecasts immediate retracement in three waves to xb, and eventually lower prices than xe. The first retracement was composed of three waves as shown in Figure 66, which confirms lower levels. The zigzag A-B-C in Figure 64 indicates that the correction subsequent to C in Figure 65 will be a flat or triangle. The triangle shown in Figure 51 reconfirms lower levels as per Figure 66, February to March, 1938.

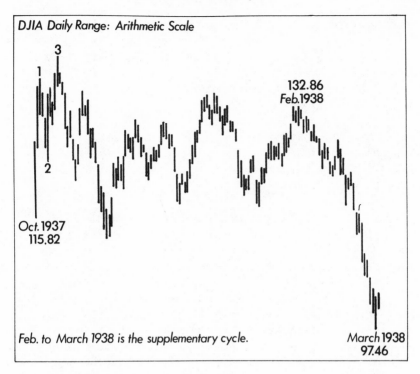

DJIA Daily Range: Arithmetic Scale

132.86
Feb. 1938

Oct. 1937
115.82

Feb. to March 1938 is the supplementary cycle.

March 1938
97.46

Figure 66

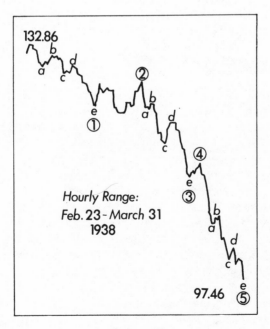

132.86

Hourly Range:
Feb. 23 - March 31
1938

97.46

Figure 67

Half Moon[43]

This is a name given to the pattern which developed between Febrary 23 and March 31, 1938, 132 to 98. It curved downward and at bottom almost perpendicular (see Figures 66 and 67).

The extension down to 115.82 (refer to Figure 65) forecast this lower level. The first advance, from 115.82, being composed of three waves, confirmed. The triangle reconfirmed.

The same pattern occurred in April, 1936, 163 to 141. Both were retracements of extensions. On account of the high speed it is necessary to recur to the hourly record, especially during the latter half.

From September to November, 1929, wave one from 381 to 195 was extended and immediately retraced in 1930. No extensions appeared in waves three or five because one occurred in wave one as just described (see Figure 19, arithmetic scale). If the extension had occurred in wave five instead of wave one during 1932, the appearance of the decline from September 1929 to July 1932 would have been the same as the "half moon" of February-March 1938.

Supplementary Cycles[44]

Insofar as records disclose, 1938 witnessed the first Industrial Supplementary Cycle (see Figures 66 and 67), February 23 to March 31, 1938, 132 to 98.

---

[43] These comments are important in predicting the speed of corrections. Unfortunately Elliott never expanded on these thoughts in later writings.

[44] Elliott's use of this term is confusing initially. He doesn't define it, and fails to illustrate his thoughts completely. What he is saying is that where he expected an A-B-C bear market, he got five waves down instead. His "supplementary cycle" is merely the fifth wave of a five-wave count, whereas at the time of writing he felt that it was somehow an additional decline following an A-B-C correction, forecast (correctly) by the characteristics of the preceding phase of decline.

Heretofore termination of wave "C" with five waves has been the end of major corrections, as in 1932.[45] This same phenomenon occurred in the Rails and Utilities between December, 1934 and March, 1935.

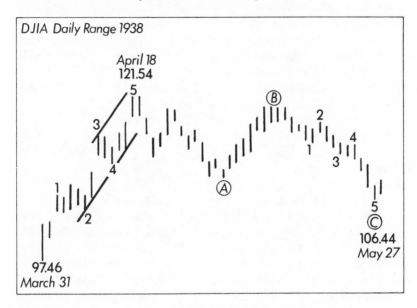

Figure 68

The movement from 97.46 to 121.54 (see Figure 68) is composed of five waves and is the first upward five wave pattern of this degree since March 1937 and confirms that 97.46 of March 31 was the bottom of wave A of the bear market.[46]

The 106.44 level of May 27 is the end of a typical flat correction from 121.54.

<hr>

[45] The 1937-1938 decline forms a clear five-wave pattern (see Figure 63), which marks only wave A of a much larger A-B-C bear market. While this fact seems to elude Elliott in these paragraphs, other sentences clearly indicate otherwise. In two instances (the first page of the book, and the final sentences in this chapter which were originally placed with Figure 68), he makes it clear that he recognizes the correct interpretation. It appears that he is actually giving two different interpretations of the 1937-38 bear market in this book. Perhaps he recognized the correct interpretation as the book was going to press

THE WAVE PRINCIPLE IN OTHER FIELDS

For years the word "cycle" has been in common use, but always in a rather loose manner implying merely a broad upward and downward movement. Thus, as concerns the course of trade in the United States, some economists refer to the period 1921-1932 as a completed cycle; others, that the period contained three cycles of lesser or greater intensity -- the movement from early 1921 to mid-1924, from 1924 to late 1927, from 1927 to mid-1932. In general the cycle has been recognized in a rough way, largely for the reason that, in its extreme aspects, it necessarily intrudes on our plans and opinions, but the underlying law of the cycle has eluded the observer.

This treatise, using the stock market as but one illustration, has dealt with the law of the cycle, and in the disclosure has shown how one cycle becomes but the starting point of another, or larger, movement that, itself, is a part of and subject to the same law as the lesser movement. This is entirely consonant with every study of Nature, for we know that She has ever unfolded in an upward direction, but always in an orderly progression. Underlying this progression, however, in whatever field, is a fixed and controlling principle, or the master rule under which Nature works. It has been the purpose of this volume, first to present the law, and then to show its practical application in one of the most baffling fields of analytical research.

Merely as cursory examples of the operation of the Wave Principle in other fields, we have presented some graphs herein, chosen at random, which readily

---

and made some quick references to his new thoughts on the first and final pages. On the other hand, perhaps he had the correct interpretation at the time of writing, but inadvertently included his previous incorrect notes when he inserted Chapter IX, describing additional formations, into Collins' manuscript.

[46] In nearly the last words of the book, Elliott correctly concludes that the March 31, 1938 low was only wave A of a large A-B-C bear market. This interpretation is the correct one, and forecasts the lower low in 1942.

illustrate that the law is at work wherever motion exists
(see charts 69 through 78). It is recommended that this
subject be given further attention by students in fields of
activity outside the stock market, as it should simplify
and clarify their particular work.

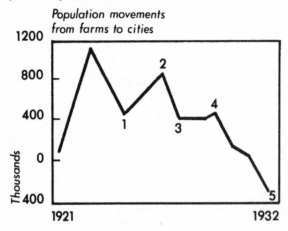

Figure 69

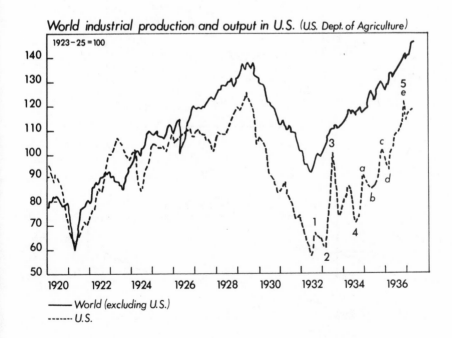

Figure 70

Prices of farm products (Bureau of Labor)

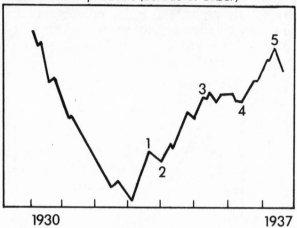

Figure 71

New paid – for life insurance

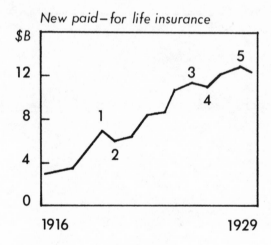

Figure 72

Gasoline consumption in the U.S.

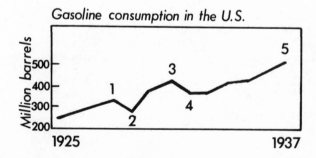

Figure 73

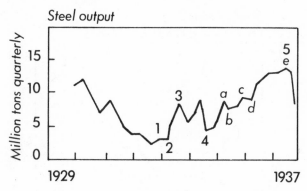

Figure 74

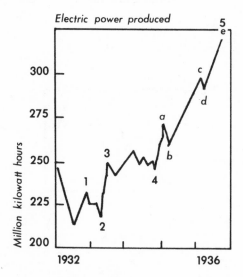

Figure 75

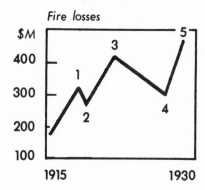

Figure 76

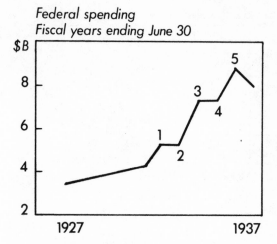

Figure 77

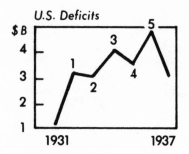

Figure 78

By no means do cycles of different items top and bottom together. Two or more may top together but bottom on widely different dates, or vice versa. A few items are noted below:

	Orthodox Tops	Bottoms
Stocks	1928 (not 1929)	1932
Bonds	1928	1932
Production Acitivity	1920	1933
Commodities	1920	1932/33
Real Estate	1923	1933
Volume Ratio	1928	June 18, 1938
N.Y.S.E. Seats	1928	June 15, 1938

After bottoming in 1932, bonds made an orthodox top in April 1934, at which time stocks would
probably have topped likewise but for the N.R.A.
Following the orthodox top in 1934 bonds described an
immense "irregular" correction with wave "B" topping in
December 1936, then bottoming in wave "C" with stocks
in March 1938.

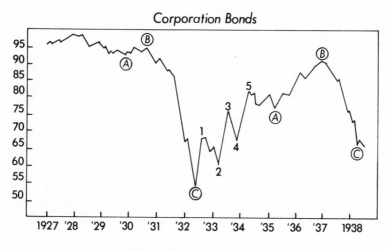

Figure 79

THE
FINANCIAL WORLD
ARTICLES

ANNOUNCING "THE WAVE PRINCIPLE"

A few months ago Mr. R. N. Elliott presented to us for consideration the results of his studies which led to the discovery of a phenomenon in human activity which may be observed most readily in stock market cycles. Believing that our readers should be informed of new developments in the art of interpretation of stock market movements, we have arranged with him to prepare a series of articles on the principle which he has discovered, the first of which will appear in the next issue of The Financial World. Many years of Mr. Elliott's career were spent in Latin America, where he served as an accountant and in other capacities in the railroading profession, and in 1927 he retired to Los Angeles, California. At that time the stock market attracted his attention. He studied economics and many "systems," charts and theories of market interpretation and forecasting. Expressions current then as now, such as "resistance levels," "double bottoms," "head and shoulders," "trend lines," etc., were examined but the significance of their applications was found to be limited. However, the possible implications of the word "cycle," which was applied rather vaguely in stock market studies, excited his curiosity. In 1934, he began to notice certain duplications of patterns which were similar in both large and small movements. This eventually resulted in his discovery, which he has named "The Wave Principle."

After investigation, we became convinced that a series of articles on this subject would be interesting and instructive to our subscribers. We leave to the individual reader a determination of the value of Mr. Elliott's principle as a basis for market forecasting, but believe that it is likely to prove at least a useful check on conclusions based upon economic considerations.

-- The Editors

—Falcofoto

R. N. Elliott

Introducing "The Wave Principle"

By R. N. Elliott

D URING the past seven or eight years, publishers of financial magazines and organizations in the investment advisory field have been virtually flooded with "systems" for which their proponents have claimed great accuracy in forecasting stock market movements. Some of them appeared to work for a while. It was immediately obvious that others had no value whatever. All have been looked upon by THE FINANCIAL WORLD with great scepticism. But after investigation of Mr. R. N. Elliott's Wave Principle THE FINANCIAL WORLD became convinced that a series of articles on this subject would be interesting and instructive to its readers. To the individual reader is left the determination of the value of the Wave Principle as a working tool in market forecasting, but it is believed that it should prove at least a useful check upon conclusions based on economic considerations.
—*The Editors.*

SINCE the beginning of time, rhythmic regularity has been the law of creation. Gradually man has acquired knowledge and power from studying the various manifestations of this law. The effects of the law are discernible in the behavior of the heavenly bodies, cyclones, day and night, even life and death! This rhythmic regularity is called a cycle.

Historical Significance

The first great advance in the scientific application of the law was made in the time of Columbus by Leonardo da Vinci in his illuminating study of the behavior of waves. Other great men followed with special applications: Halley with his comet, Bell with sound waves, Edison with electrical waves, Marconi with radio waves, and still others with waves of psychology, cosmic waves, television, etc. One thing in common that all these waves or forms of energy have is their cyclical behavior or ability to repeat themselves indefinitely. This cyclical behavior is characterized by two forces — one building up and the other tearing down. Today Hitler is said to be timing his conquests in accordance with this natural law as interpreted in the movements of the stars — but the destructive forces are accumulating and at the proper time will become dominant—completing the cycle.

Because of this phenomenon of repetition or rhythmic recurrence, it is possible to apply the lesson learned from other manifestations of the law in a very practical and profitable way. The trade cycle and the bull and bear movements of the stock market are also governed by the same natural law. Some fifty years ago Charles Dow through his observations of the important changes in the stock market gradually built up the Dow Theory, which now is accepted in many quarters as having special forecasting significance. Since Dow's studies, the store of information regarding market transactions has been greatly multiplied, and important and valuable new forecasting inferences can be drawn from certain behavior.

Through a long illness the writer had the opportunity to study the available information concerning stock market behavior. Gradually the wild, senseless and apparently uncontrollable changes in prices from year to year, from month to month, or from day to day, linked themselves into a law-abiding rhythmic pattern of waves. This pattern seems to repeat itself over and over again. With knowledge of this law or phenomenon (that I have called the Wave Principle) it is possible to measure and forecast the various trends and corrections (minor, intermediate, major and even movements of a still greater degree) that go to complete a great cycle.

Fig. 1

This phenomenon is disclosed in Figure 1. The full wave or progressive phase of the cycle consists of five impulses: three moving forward and two moving downward. Waves 1, 3 and 5 are in the direction of the main trend. Wave 2 corrects Wave 1— and Wave 4 corrects Wave 3. Usually the three forward movements are in approximately parallel planes; this may also be true of Waves 2 and 4.

Fig. 2

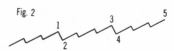

Each of the three primary waves that together make a completed movement is divided into five waves of the next smaller or intermediate degree. This subdivision is shown in Figure 2. Note carefully that there are five smaller or intermediate waves making

PART I

INTRODUCING "THE WAVE PRINCIPLE"

Since the beginning of time, rhythmic regularity has been the law of creation. Gradually man has acquired knowledge and power from studying the various manifestations of this law. The effects of the law are discernible in the behavior of the tides, the heavenly bodies, cyclones, day and night, even life and death. This rhythmic regularity is called a cycle.

Historical Significance

The first great advance in the scientific application of the law was made in the time of Columbus by Leonardo da Vinci in his illuminating study of the behavior of waves. Other great men followed with special applications: Halley with his comet, Bell with sound waves, Edison with electrical waves, Marconi with radio waves, and still others with waves of psychology, cosmic waves, television, etc. One thing in common that all these waves or forms of energy have is their cyclical behavior or ability to repeat themselves indefinitely. This cyclical behavior is characterized by two forces -- one building up and the other tearing down. Today Hitler is said to be timing his conquests in accordance with this natural law as interpreted in the movements of the stars -- but the destructive forces are accumulating and at the proper time will become dominant, completing the cycle.

Because of this phenomenon of repetition or rhythmic recurrence, it is possible to apply the lesson learned from other manifestations of the law in a very practical and profitable way. The trade cycle and the bull and bear movements of the stock market are also governed by the same natural law. Some fifty years ago Charles Dow, through his observations of the important changes in the stock market, gradually built up the Dow Theory, which now is accepted in many quarters as having special forecasting significance. Since Dow's studies, the store of information regarding market transactions has been greatly multiplied, and important and valuable new forecasting inferences can be drawn from certain behavior.

Through a long illness the writer had the

opportunity to study the available information concerning stock market behavior. Gradually the wild, senseless and apparently uncontrollable changes in prices from year to year, from month to month, or from day to day, linked themselves into a law-abiding rhythmic pattern of waves. This pattern seems to repeat itself over and over again. With knowledge of this law or phenomenon (that I have called the Wave Principle) it is possible to measure and forecast the various trends and corrections (minor, intermediate, major and even movements of a still greater degree) that go to complete a great cycle.

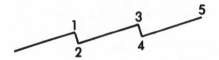

Figure 1

This phenomenon is disclosed in Figure 1. The full wave or progressive phase of the cycle consists of five impulses: three moving forward and two moving downward. Waves 1, 3 and 5 are in the direction of the main trend. Wave 2 corrects Wave 1 and Wave 4 corrects Wave 3. Usually the three forward movements are in approximately parallel planes; this may also be true of Waves 2 and 4.

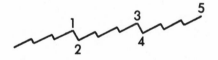

Figure 2

Each of the three primary waves that together make a completed movement is divided into five waves of the next smaller or intermediate degree. This subdivision is shown in Figure 2. Note carefully that there are five smaller or intermediate waves making up the Primary Wave 1, five in Primary Wave 3, and five in Primary Wave 5. The Primary Wave 2 corrects the completed Primary Wave 1 consisting of five Intermediate waves; Wave 4 in turn corrects the five Intermediate waves that make up Primary Wave 3.

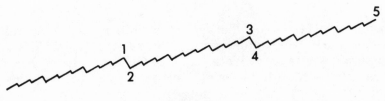

Figure 3

Each Intermediate forward wave is in turn divided into five Minor waves as shown in Figure 3. When the fifth Minor wave of the fifth Intermediate phase of the fifth Primary movement has spend its force, a formidable top has been constructed. Upon completion of a movement of this magnitude, the destructive forces become dominant; the primary trend turns downward and a bear market is in progress long before the economic, political or financial reasons for the change in outlook are clearly apparent.

PART II

In the preceding discussion of the Wave Principle as applied to the forecasting of stock price movements, it was pointed out that a completed movement consists of five waves, and that a set of five waves of one degree completes the first wave of the next higher degree. When Wave 5 of any degree has been completed, there should occur a correction that will be more severe than any previous correction in the cyclical movement.

Completed Movement

The rhythm of the corrective phases is different from that of the waves moving in the direction of the main trend. These corrective vibrations, or Waves 2 and 4, are each made up of <u>three</u> lesser waves, whereas the progressive waves (1, 3 and 5) are each composed of <u>five</u> smaller impulses. In Figure 4, the completed movement is shown, being identical to Figure 3 except that Waves 2 and 4 of the "zigzag" pattern are shown in greater detail. These Waves 2 and 4 are thus shown to consist each of three component phases but as these two waves are also "completed movements," they are also characterized by <u>five-wave</u> impulses; that is, the "a" and "c" phases (the first and third movements of the correction) are also each composed of five smaller waves, while "b" (the correction of the correction) is composed of three lesser waves. This question of corrections will require more extended discussion later on, as some forms and types are so complicated in structure that their presentation at this stage might be confusing.

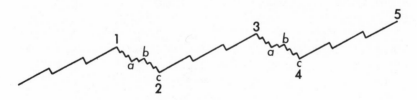

Figure 4

The student using the Wave Principle to forecast price changes does not require confirmation by a companion average, inasmuch as the Principle applies to individual stocks, to various groups (steels, rails, utilities, coppers, oils, etc.) and also to commodities and the various "averages," such as those of Dow-Jones, Standard Statistics, New York Times, New York Herald Tribune, the Financial Times of London, etc. At any given time it will be found that some stocks are advancing and others are declining, but the great majority of individual stocks will be following the same pattern at the same time. It is for this reason that the wave pattern of the averages will correctly reflect the cyclical position of the market as a whole. The larger the number of stocks included in an average, the more sharply outlined the wave impressions will be. This means that if stocks are widely distributed among a large number of individuals, the response to cyclical influences will be registered more definitely and rhythmically than if the distribuition is limited.

Price Ranges Used

No reliance can be placed on "closings," daily or weekly. It is the highest and lowest ranges that guide the subsequent course of the cycle. In fact it was only due to the establishment and publication by Dow-Jones of the "daily range" in 1928 and of the "hourly range" in 1932 that sufficient reliable data became available to establish the rhythmic recurrence of the phenomenon that I have called the Wave Principle. It is the series of actual "travels" by the market, hourly, daily and weekly, that reveal the rhythmic forces in their entirety. The "closings" do not disclose the full story, and it is for this reason (lack of detailed data) that the phase-by-phase course of the London stock market is more difficult to predict than the New York market.

The complete measurement of the length of a wave is therefore its continuous travel between two corrections of the same or greater degree. The length of a wave of the lowest degree is its travel in one direction without any sort of correction even in the hourly record.[1] After two corrections have appeared in the hourly record, the movement then enters its fifth and last stage, or third impulse. So-called "resistance" levels and other technical considerations have but little value in forecasting or measuring the length or duration of these

---

[1] When a minute-by-minute record is available, even smaller waves are quite discernible.

waves.

Outside Influences

As the Wave Principle forecasts the different phases or segments of a cycle, the experienced student will find that current news or happenings, or even decrees or acts of government, seem to have but little effect, if any, upon the course of the cycle. It is true that sometimes unexpected news or sudden events, particularly those of a highly emotional nature, may extend or curtail the length of travel between corrections, but the number of waves or underlying rhythmic regularity of the market remains constant. It even seems to be more logical to conclude that the cyclical derangement of trade, bringing widespread social unrest, is the cause of wars, rather than that cycles are produced by wars.

PART III

Because, after the fifth wave of an advancing movement has been completed, the correction will be more severe than any yet experienced in the cycle, it is desirable to determine beforehand where the top of this wave will be. With such knowledge, the investor can take the necessary steps to assume a defensive policy and convert profits into cash under the most favorable market conditions. He will also be in a strong position to repurchase with confidence when the correction has run its course.

The previous article stated that "The complete measurement of the length of a wave is therefore its continuous travel between two corrections of the same or greater degree." By repeatedly measuring the length of these waves as they develop, under a method known as channeling, it is possible to determine at the time of completion of Wave 4 approximately where Wave 5 should "top."

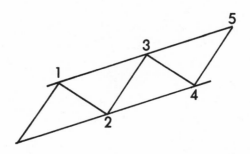

Figure 6

Figure 6[2] shows a normal completed movement or "cycle," in which Waves 1, 3 and 5 each have approximately the same length. Forecasting the ultimate movement by the channeling method must wait until Waves 1 and 2 have been completed. At such time it is possible to ascertain the "base line" for the lower limits of the channel by extending a straight line from the starting point of Wave 1 through the stopping point of Wave 2. This is shown in Figure 7. Wave 3, normally parallel to Wave 1, should end in the approximate vicinity

2 By error of omission, no chart labeled "Figure 5" appeared in the articles.

of the tentative or dashed upper line of the channel.

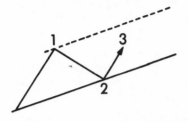

Figure 7

This tentative upper line is drawn parallel to the base line from the top of Wave 1 and extended forward. But conditions may be so favorable that Wave 3 takes on temporary strength and exceeds the normal theoretical expectation, as shown in Figure 8.

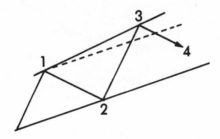

Figure 8

When Wave 3 has ended, the actual upper channel line is drawn from the top of Wave 1 through the top of Wave 3. And for forecasting the bottom of Wave 4 reaction, a tentative or dashed base line is drawn from the bottom of Wave 2 parallel to the actual Wave 1-Wave

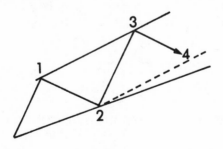

Figure 9

3 upper channel line. In Figure 9 the theoretical expectancy for termination of Wave 4 is shown, as well as the actual termination.

With the second reaction, or Wave 4, terminated, the final and all-important channeling step can be taken. The base line of the channel is extended across the stopping points of the two reactionary phases (Waves 2 and 4), and a parallel upper line is drawn across the top of Wave 3. Wave 1 is desregarded entirely, unless Wave 3 was exceptionally strong.[3] When the base and upper parallel lines are drawn as suggested, the approximate termination of Wave 5 will be forecast, as shown in Figure 10.

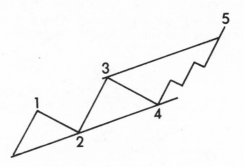

Figure 10

This channeling method is, of course, subordinate in importance to the rhythm of the various phases that make up the completed movement. Waves 1, 3 and 5 should each be composed of five waves of the next lower degree. Theoretically Wave 5 should wind up at about the intersection with the upper parallel line drawn as above described. Sometimes, however, Wave 5 develops excessive strength. Patterns in which this "throw-over" should occur will be discussed in subsequent articles.

---

[3] Elliott seems to be referring to a phenomenon I have noticed whereby when wave three is abnormally strong, almost verical, the correct channel for marking the end of wave five is constructed by drawing an upper channel line which touches the peak of wave one and cuts through wave three. Frost and I illustrate this idea in ELLIOTT WAVE PRICIPLE -- KEY TO STOCK MARKET PROFITS.

PART IV

A completed price movement has been shown to consist of five waves, with the entire movement representing the first wave of the next larger degree. By classifying the degree of the various phases, it is possible to determine the relative position of the market at all times as well as the economic changes that should follow.[4]

The longest reliable record of American stock prices is the Axe-Houghton Index (published in The New York Times Annalist) dating from 1854. Long range forecasting under the Wave Principle must therefore start with the completion of the bear market that terminated in 1857. The great tidal movement that commenced in 1857 and ended on November 28, 1928, (the orthodox top) represents one wave of a cycle of the largest degree. Whether this extended movement was the first, third or fifth wave of the Grand Super Cycle necessarily depends upon what happened previous to 1857. By breaking this historic wave down into its component series of five-wave movements, and by breaking in turn the fifth wave of the next smaller degree into its five waves, the student will have actual examples of the various degrees that markets traverse. To avoid confusion in classifying the various degrees of market movements, it is suggested that the names and symbols devised below be used in their respective order (see table, next page).

The longest of these waves lasted for over seventy years and included a long series of "bull" and "bear" markets. But it is the combination of the smaller hourly, daily and weekly rhythms that complete and measure the important Intermediate and Primary cycles that are of great practical importance to every investor.

When the Dow-Jones Industrial Average reached 295.62 on November 28, 1928, the price movement completed the fifth Minuette impulse of the fifth Minute wave of the fifth Minor phase of the fifth Intermediate movement of the fifth Primary trend in the fifth Cycle of the fifth Super Cycle in Wave 1, 3 or 5 of the Grand Super Cycle. For that reason, although the actual top of 386.10 was not reached until September 3,

---

[4] Only a true technician would make this comment.

Degree of Movement	Symbol and Wave No.	Duration
Grand Super Cycle:	gsc I (?).............	1857-1928

Super Cycle......	sc I...................	1857-1864
	sc II.................	1864-1877
	sc III...............	1877-1881
	sc IV................	1881-1896
	sc V.................	1896-1928

Cycle...........	c I..................	1896-1899
	c II	1899-1907
	c III...............	1907-1909
	c IV................	1909-1921
	c V.................	1921-1928

Primary.........	((I)).....June,	1921-Mar., 1923
	((II))....Mar.,	1923-May, 1924
	((III))...May,	1924-Nov., 1925
	((IV))....Nov.,	1925-Mar., 1926
	((V)).....Mar.,	1926-Nov., 1928

Intermediate... (I)-(V)		Price movements illus-
Minor..............I-V		trating the Intermedi-
Minute.............1-5		ate and smaller de-
Minuette...........A-E		grees will be discussed
Sub-Minuette.......a-e		in subsequent articles.

1929, the point reached on November 28, 1928, is designated as the "orthodox" top. This may sound confusing to most readers, but the patterns in which "irregular tops" higher than "orthodox tops" occur will be discussed in due course.

PART V

The scope and duration of any price movement are influenced by what happened in the previous cycle of similar or larger degree. The movement that started in 1896 and took thirty-three years to complete, culminating on September 3, 1929, at 386.10, was so dynamic that the corrective bear cycle was correspondingly severe.

Orderly Decline

Within less than three years, prices were reduced to 10.5 per cent of the peak level. Despite its high speed, the downward course of the bear cycle followed a well-defined and rhythmic pattern of waves. Furthermore, it kept within the limits of the pre-measured channel. It was, therefore, possible to determine beforehand approximately where the bear market would end and the new bull market begin. Because of the amplitude of the previous cycles, the new bull market would necessarily be of a large degree, lasting for years. When taking a position for such a movement, the long term investor would be warranted in maintaining his investments until the end of the fifth major wave was in measurable sight. From that point he should be extremely careful.

Previous discussions have dealt with the fundamental theory of the Wave Principle. It is now appropriate to show the application of the theory to an actual market. In Figure 11, the completed five-wave movement of the extreme monthly price ranges of the Dow-Jones Industrial Average from July 8, 1932 to March 10, 1937, is charted arithmetically. The series of Minuette, Minute, Minor and Intermediate waves all resolved themselves -- in the monthly, weekly, daily and hourly records -- to form and complete each of the five Primary waves. Waves ((I)), ((III)) and ((V)) were each composed of three distinct phases, as shown by the A-B-C patterns. The extent and duration of each important phase are shown in the accompanying table.

When Wave ((IV)) is finished and Wave ((V)) is under way, much closer attention to the market is required. Accordingly the channel was carefully noted. A base line was drawn from the bottom of Wave ((II)) through the bottom of Wave ((IV)), and an upper line

parallel thereto was extended forward from the top of
Wave ((III)). See the accompanying table and chart.

Phases of the Primary Movement 1932-1937

Wave ((I)) from 40.56 July 8, 1932 to completion of
Wave ((V)) at 195.59 on March 10, 1937. (Dow Jones
Industrial Monthly Averages).

WAVE	FROM				TO			
((I)).....	40.56	July	8,	1932-	81.39	Sept.	8,	1932
((II))....	81.39	Sept.	8,	1932-	49.68	Feb.	27,	1933
A......	81.39	Sept.	8,	1932-	55.04	Dec.	3,	1932
B......	55.04	Dec.	3,	1932-	65.28	Jan.	11,	1933
C......	65.28	Jan.	11,	1933-	49.68	Feb.	27,	1933
((III))...	49.68	Feb.	27,	1933-	110.53	July	18,	1933
((IV))....	110.53	July	18,	1933-	84.58	July	26,	1934
A......	110.53	July	18,	1933-	82.20	Oct.	21,	1933
B......	82.20	Oct.	21,	1933-	111.93	Feb.	5,	1934
C......	111.93	Feb.	5,	1934-	84.58	July	26,	1934
((V)).....	84.58	July	26,	1934-	195.59	Mar.	10,	1937

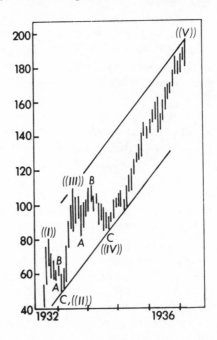

Figure 11

Bearish Indication?

          In November 1936, immediately after the
President was reelected by an overwhelming majority
vote, external conditions appeared to be so favorable for
the bull market that it was extremely difficult even to
think of being bearish. Yet according to the Wave
Principle, the bull market even then was in its final
stage. The long term movement that started in 1932 had
by November 12, 1936, reached 185.52, and the various
five-wave advances of the preceding 53 months were in
the culminating stage of the Primary degree. Note how
close the price level was to the upper part of the channel
at that time. Yet it required another four months to
complete the pattern.

          The final and relatively insignificant wave,
necessary to confirm that the end was at hand, developed
during the week ended Wednesday, March 10, 1937. In
that week both the Industrial and Rail averages moved
forward on huge volume to a moderately higher recovery
level, and according to one of the most widely followed
market theories thereby "reaffirmed that the major trend
was upward."

          The Industrials reached 195.59 -- compared
with the November 1929 panic bottom of 195.35 and the
February 1931 rally top of 196.96.[5] In that week the
advancing prices met the top of the channel. The
President's remarks about prices for copper and steel
being too high did not take place until April, and by that
time the bear movement was well under way.

---

[5] Elliott recognized this type of support/resistance level
in the averages. The market often chooses levels around
which to turn continually or to break only dramatically.
Usually these levels have something to do with Fibonacci
relationships. Look closely at the 740 level, the 780 level,
the 847 level and the 995 level on a chart of the recent
history of the Dow.

PART VI

In the 1932-1937 Primary bull movement (see Fig. 11, Part V), Waves ((I)) and ((III)) ran at high speed. Naturally they terminated in a short time. But Wave ((V)) was so gradual and orderly that it lasted longer than the time interval required for the previous four waves combined. In the discussion of this movement, it was stated that by November 1936 it was evident that the bull market was in an extremely advanced stage, but that it required another four months to complete the pattern. Although the largest phases of the fifth Primary were in the culminating stage, the smallest component phases (Minuette, etc.) were still developing.

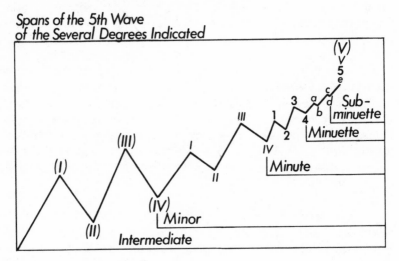

Figure 12

Figure 12 illustrates how the fifth wave of an important degree becomes extended by the development of five waves of the next smaller degree, and five more of a still smaller degree. Thus, an Intermediate trend will end on the fifth Sub-Minuette impulse of the fifth Minuette wave of the fifth Minute phase of the fifth Minor movement of the fifth Intermediate swing. Note that as Wave (V) advances, the corrections tend to become smaller and of shorter duration. Compare with 1935-1937. The termination of a fifth wave marks the point at which an entire movement of the same degree is to be corrected by a reverse movement of similar degree.

Confusion in the identification of the waves of

the smaller degrees, developing toward the end of the fifth wave of the important degree, is sometimes caused by "throw-overs." A throw-over is a penetration in an advancing movement of the upper parallel line of the channel (see Part III), and in a declining movement of the lower parallel line of the channel. Volume tends to rise on a throw-over, and should be very heavy as applied to the fifth Intermediate wave of a Primary movement. Failure of the fifth wave of any degree to penetrate the channel line, accompanied by indications of a sustained decline, is a warning of weakness. The extent of the weakness depends upon the degree of the wave. Sometimes, such weakness furnishes a new base for the recommencement of the fifth wave. Throw-overs are also caused by the scale of the chart study of the movement. They are more likely to occur in an advancing movement on arithmetic scales, and in declining movements on logarithmic scales.

Sometimes the fifth wave will "stretch"[6] -- that is, deploy or spread out. The fifth wave, instead of proceeding in the normal one-wave pattern of the same degree as the movement as a whole, simply stretches or sub-divides into five waves of lower degree. In rhythmic forecasting, this stretching applies to the fifth wave itself, rather than to the terminating cycle of which it is a part. Such spreading out is a characteristic of markets that are unusually strong (or weak, if a down movement). An example of stretching occurred in the 1921-1928 upswing, representing the culmination of a 72-year advance.

---

[6] This idea of "stretching" in a fifth wave is analogous to the extension idea when smaller and smaller degrees of third waves extend, surrounding the midpoint of a wave, usually the point of maximum thrust.

PART VII

The rhythm of corrective movements is the most difficult feature of the Wave Principle. Intensive study of detail of the correction will sometimes be necessary in order to determine the position of the market and the outlook. Mastery of the subject, however, should prove extremely profitable. All corrections are characterized by <u>three</u> broad waves, but the detail and extent can vary considerably, and thus different patterns are formed. Various factors (time, rate of speed, extent of previous movement, volume, news items, etc.) tend to influence and shape the corrective pattern. Based on the writer's market research and experience, there appear to be four main types or patterns of corrections. These types have been designated as Zig-zag, Flat, Irregular and Triangle. Discussion of the triangle, in its various forms, must be presented in a separate article. The other three forms are diagrammed in Figures 13, 14 and 15.

Small corrections that run their course in a comparatively short time are exemplified in Figure 13. Corrections of a larger degree are described in Figure 14. Figure 15 affords a diagram of the market action when the Primary or Intermediate trends turn downward. Some of these corrections, particularly those of the irregular type, may extend over a period of years and embrace movements that are commonly mistaken for "bull markets."

The three-wave or A-B-C formations that characterize the zig-zag, flat and irregular corrections are clearly shown in the accompanying diagrams. The zig-zag type was discussed briefly in Part II (Figure 4). It differs from other corrections in that both the first and third waves (A and C) are composed of five smaller vibrations. The second (B) wave of zig-zag corrections is composed of three impulses. Sometimes, in high-speed movement, the first leg (A) may appear continuous, and resort to the smaller or hourly studies may be necessary to detect the flow.

The first and second waves of both flats and irregulars each consist of <u>three</u> vibrations of a degree smaller than that of the previous movement. Of the three movements making up the second or "B" phase of both flats and irregulars, the first and third (a and c) are each

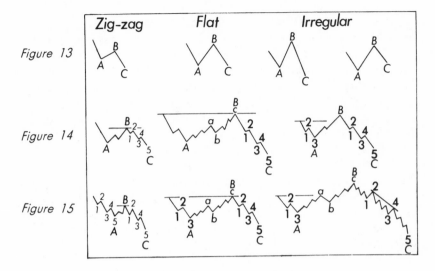

composed of <u>five</u> still smaller impulses. In a flat all of the three waves have approximately the same length.

An irregular correction is distinguished by the fact that the second or "B" wave advances to a secondary top higher than the orthodox top established in the primary movement. Liquidation in the third or "C" wave is therefore usually more intensive than in the first phase. Normally C terminates below the bottom of A, although there are instances of C, the third phase, being abbreviated. In the larger and important corrections, such as Primary and Intermediate, the "C" or third phase of the irregular correction may consist of <u>three smaller five-wave sets,</u> as shown in Figure 15.

By analyzing and placing the type of correction that is being experienced, the student has a basis for determining both the extent of the correction and the extent of the following movement. Channeling (see Part III) can help in determining the extent. The application of these corrective patterns to specific markets will be shown and discussed in subsequent articles.

PART VIII

Triangular corrections are protracted trend hesitations. The main movement may have gone too far and too fast in relation to the slower economic processes, and prices proceed to mark time until the underlying forces catch up. Triangles have lasted as long as nine months and have been as short as seven hours. There are two classes of triangles, horizontal and diagonal. These are shown in Figures 16 and 17.

The four types of horizontal triangles are Ascending, Descending, Symmetrical and the rare Reverse Symmetrical. In the last named the apex is the beginning of the triangular correction. In the other forms the apex is the end of the correction, which, however, may terminate before the apex is actually reached.

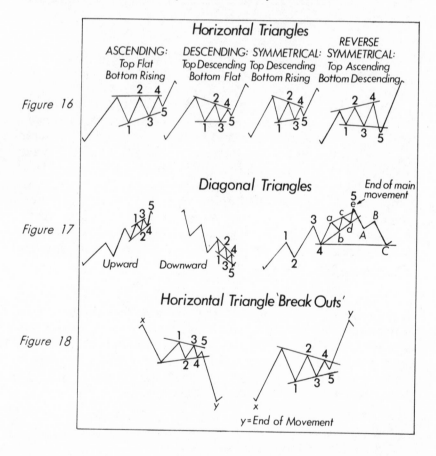

Figure 16

Figure 17

Figure 18

All triangles contain five waves or legs, each of which is composed of not more than three lesser waves. Outlines that do not conform to this definition fall outside the law of the Wave Principle. All waves in a triangle must be part of a movement in one direction; otherwise, the "triangle" is only a coincidence.

The entire travel within the triangle represents a wave of the main movement. The horizontal triangle occurs as Wave 2 or Wave 4. If it occurs as Wave 2, the main movement will have only three waves. At the conclusion of a horizontal triangle, the market will resume the trend that was interrupted by the triangle, and the direction of that trend will be the same as that of triangular Wave 2. The "break-out" from the horizontal triangle (in the direction of triangular Wave 2) will usually be fast and represent the final wave of the main movement, and be followed by reversal of the trend. The extent of the "break-out" will usually approximate the distance between the widest parts of the triangle. The diagrams in Figure 18 illustrate the "break-out" from horizontal triangles.

Diagonal triangles are either upward or downward. They can occur as either Wave 3 or Wave 5 of the main movement.[7] Usually they occur as Wave 5, and are preceded by four main waves. But the completion of the diagonal triangle represents the end of the main movement. The second wave within the diagonal triangle will be in the direction opposite to that of the main movement, and will indicate the direction of the reversal to follow conclusion of the triangle. At the conclusion of the fifth wave in this form of triangle, the rapid reversal of trend will usually retrun the market to about the level from which the triangle started (see Figure 17, third diagram).

Triangles are not apparent in all studies. Sometimes they will appear in the weekly scale, but will

---

[7] Based on the discussion of diagonal triangles in The Wave Principle, this comment is almost assuredly unintentional. Diagonal triangles never occur as wave three. Third waves are characteristically strong, while fifths are terminal movements.

not be visible in the daily. Sometimes they are present in, say, The New York Times average and not in another average. Thus, the broad and important movement from October 1937 to February 1938 formed a triangle in the Standard Statistics weekly range, but was not visible in other averages; the second wave of this triangle pointed downward; the fifth wave culminated on February 23; the drastic March break followed.

PART IX

The "extension," though not frequent, is one of the most important market phenomena measureable by the Wave Principle. In an extension the length (and degree)[8] of the wave becomes much larger than normal. It may occur as a part of Wave 1 or 3, but is usually a part of Wave 5 of the main movement.[9] The extended movement is composed of the normal five-wave phase, followed by a three-wave retracing correction, and then by a second advancing movement in three phases. Of the normal five waves, the fifth vibration is usually the largest and most dynamic of the series,[10] thus becoming, in effect, an extension of the extension.

A warning of the approach of this dynamic phase of Wave 5 is conveyed when Waves 1 and 3 are short and regular and confined within the channel,[11] and when the first corrective vibration of the extension is completed near the top of the channel. The length of important extensions may be several times the breadth of the original channel.

Channelling is also useful in measuring the travel of the extension. Thus, in Figures 19 and 20, the line "b-d" represents the base line, and the dashed upper parallel line "c-e" measures the normal expectancy for the "first top" of the extension.

The completion of the normal or first five waves of an extension is never the end of the cyclical movement, but does constitute a distinct warning that the bull cycle is approaching an end, as only two more broad waves (one down and one up) would fully reflect the maximum force of the bull market.

---

[8] The size of an extended wave is larger, but the degree (Minor, Intermediate or Primary) is the same as that of the two non-extended waves.
[9] See footnote number 22 in The Wave Principle regarding this contention.
[10] Fifths can be, but third waves are most often the "largest and most dynamic of a series."
[11] Since an extension generally occurs in one of the three impulse waves, it follows that when waves 1 and 3 are short and simply constructed (as long as wave 3 is longer than wave 1), wave 5 will likely be extended.

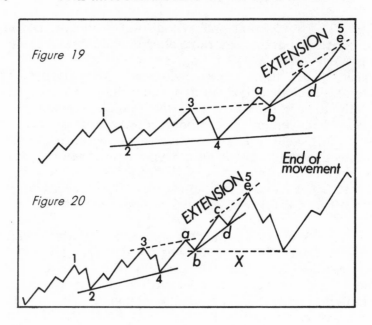

Figure 19

Figure 20

After the first five waves of the extension have been completed, a severe correction (that is usually in three waves, but may be triangular) sets in. This correction becomes Wave A of an irregular cyclical correction. Wave A generally carries the market down (breaking the extension channel) to about the beginning of the extension, although a protracted period of backing and filling[12] may serve to mitigate the severity of this corrective phase. The dashed line marked "X" in Figure 20 indicates the average expectancy for the completion of Wave A.

When Wave A has been completed, the main or cyclical movement is resumed in three broad phases that carry the market into new high ground -- even though "e" in Figures 19 and 20 may have been the "orthodox top" of a major or primary bull movement. But this new top, or "irregular top," is the final high point for the bull market. This three-wave advancing phase becomes Wave B of the irregular cyclical correction.

---

[12] The standard technical term for this type of action near a top is "distribution."

The completion of Wave B marks the beginning of Wave C of the irregular cyclical correction, that in this phase is a bear market of major importance. Wave C should carry the market down in five fast waves to about the bottom of Primary Wave IV of the preceding bull movement. Example: following the dynamic extension in 1928: Wave A, down from November to December 1928; Wave B, upward to September 1929; Wave C, downward to July 1932.

Extensions also occur in bear markets. Thus, the five waves of an extension were completed October 19, 1937, with the market reaching 115.83. They were followed, in this case, by a broad triangular correction (instead of the irregular A-B-C pattern) covering a period of four months, eventually reaching 97.46 on March 31, 1938. Wave 2 of this triangular correction was in the same direction as the downward cyclical trend.

A tremendous extension occurred in commodity price movements, particularly that of electrolytic copper, in the spring of 1937.

In individual stocks, the "orthodox top" of International Harvester was reached at 111-112 in January 1937; Wave A, in a backing and filling movement that reduced the severity of the correction, carried the stock to 109 in April; Wave B reached a new cyclical top of 120 in August (the general market topped in March), and Wave C brought the stock down to about 53 in November.

PART X

Following the completion of the bull market from 1932-1937 (see Figure 11, Part V), a three-phase cyclical correction was in order. The first phase should and did consist of five large waves. The first phase of this correction was the decline that ran from 195.59 (Dow-Jones Industrial Average) on March 10, 1937, to 97.46 on March 31, 1938.[13] The accompanying Figure 21 shows the weekly range of the market during this period, on an arithmetic scale. Despite the highly emotional nature that prevailed at certain stages, the rhythmic forecasting principle continued to function. The minute details registered in the daily and hourly patterns are, of course, not entirely visible in the weekly range. For this reason, the essential details of price and time of the five big waves making up this first cyclical phase are given:

Cyclical (A) -- from 195.59 on March 10, 1937, to 163.31 on June 17, 1937.
Cyclical Wave (B) -- from 163.31 on June 17, 1937, to 190.38 on August 14, 1937.
Cyclical Wave (C) -- from 190.38 on August 14, 1937, to 115.83 on October 19, 1937.
Cyclical Wave (D) -- from 115.83 on October 19, 1937, to 132.86 on February 23, 1938.
Cyclical Wave (E) -- from 132.86 on February 23, 1938, to 97.46 on March 31, 1938.

Cyclical Wave (A) was composed of five minor waves, as follows:

1 - 195.59 on March 10 to 179.28 on March 22.
2 - 179.28 on March 22 to 187.99 on March 31.
3 - 187.99 on March 31 to 166.20 on May 18.
4 - 166.20 on May 18 to 175.66 on June 5.
5 - 175.66 on June 5 to 163.31 on June 17.

Wave 3 in Cyclical Wave (A) was composed of five vibrations.

Cyclical Wave (B) was composed of three waves, and

[13] Here Elliott correctly forecasts that the bear market which started in 1937 was not over. The eventual low occurred four years later in 1942.

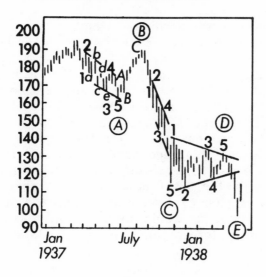

Figure 21

an "irregular top":

    A - 163.31 on June 17 to 170.46 on June 24.
    B - 170.46 on June 24 to 166.11 on June 29.
    C - 166.11 on June 29 to 187.31 on Aug. 4.

The "irregular top"[14] was completed on August 14, 1937, forecasting a severe cyclical decline.

Cyclical Wave (C) was composed of five large waves, with an extension developing in the fifth wave. Had it not been for this extension, the normal completion of the first phase of the cyclical correction would probably have been in the neighborhood of 135-140. The analysis of Wave (C) is as follows:

    1 - 190.38 on Aug. 14 to 175.09 on Aug. 27.
    2 - 175.09 on Aug. 27 to 179.10 on Aug. 31.
    3 - 179.10 on Aug. 31 to 154.94 on Sept. 13.
    4 - 154.94 on Sept. 13 to 157.12 on Sept. 30.
    5 - 157.12 on Sept. 30 to 115.83 on Oct. 19.

In Cyclical Wave (C), there were three "sets" of

---

[14] See footnote number 42 in The Wave Principle.

five vibrations in the downward trend, with the first, third and fifth minor waves each being composed of five impulses. Wave 4 was a fairly important upward correction, in the familiar A-B-C formation. The extension that developed in the fifth vibration of Wave 5 indicated that the ground thus lost would be immediately recovered, that the secondary decline would carry the market into new low ground for the cyclical correction, that following this secondary decline, the normal protracted period of backing and filling might form a triangle, with the final down thrust[15] completing the first phase of the cyclical correction, and that a very substantial recovery would follow in at least five large waves,[16] thus forecasting the 1938 March-November "bull market."

Cyclical Wave (D), as indicated by the extension that occurred in Wave (C), was composed of a huge triangle:

Triangle wave 1 - in three vibrations (A, B and C), from 115.83 on Oct. 19 to 141.22 on Oct. 29.
    A - 115.83 on Oct. 19 to 137.82 on Oct. 21.
    B - 137.82 on Oct. 21 to 124.56 on Oct. 25.
    C - 124.56 on Oct. 25 to 141.22 on Oct. 29.

2 - 141.22 on Oct. 29 to 112.54 on Nov. 23.
3 - 112.54 on Nov. 23 to 134.95 on Jan. 12.
4 - 134.95 on Jan. 12 to 117.13 on Feb. 4.
5 - 117.13 on Feb. 4 to 132.86 on Feb. 23.

None of the "legs" in this triangle was composed of more than three waves. Following the completion of the fifth wave in the triangle, the downward movement of the cyclical correction was resumed.

---

[15] I.e., wave (E).
[16] This should read, "three large waves."

Cyclical Wave (E) was composed of five lesser waves, as follows:

1 - 132.86 on Feb. 23 to 121.77 on March 12.
2 - 121.77 on March 12 to 127.44 on March 15.
3 - 127.44 on March 15 to 112.78 on March 23.
4 - 112.78 on March 23 to 114.37 on March 25.
5 - 114.37 on March 25 to 97.46 on March 31.

The first large phase of the cyclical correction of the 1932-1937 bull market was thus finally completed, and the market was ready for the second important upward phase of the cyclical correction. This correction extinguished 63.3 per cent of the 155.03 points recovered in the 1932-1937 movement.

PART XI

In using the Wave Principle as a medium for forecasting price movements, the student should recognize that there are cycles within cycles, and that each such cycle or sub-cycle must be studied and correctly placed in respect to the broad underlying movement. These sub-cyclical or corrective phases in a bull market are often important enough to be mistaken for "bear markets." The strong but sub-cyclical correction from March 31, 1938 to November 12, 1938 had a "bull pattern" of five important waves making up its first phase,[17] and was (and still is) regarded by many as a real bull market. Broadly speaking, extended rallies or corrections of bear cycles are composed of three phases, and this is also true of extensive bearish corrections of bull movements.

Wave Characteristics

The character of the waves making up an extended movement is affected by a number of factors that may seem irrelevant to the inexperienced. Examination of any completed movement seems to support the fatalistic theory that the extent or objective of the price movement is fixed or predetermined. The time of the entire cycle is also possibly fixed, but the time of the component phases appears to be variable.[18] The variations in the time cycle appear to be governed by the speed or rate of the price movement, and vice versa. Thus, if the market movement has been violent and rapid in one phase, the next corresponding phase is likely to show a marked slowing down in speed.[19] Example: The first primary wave of the 1932-1937 bull cycle advanced 40 points or 100 per cent in 9 weeks, averaging 4.4 points per week. The second bull phase advanced 60 points or 120 per cent in 20 weeks, averaging 3 points per week. The third or final phase crept forward 110 points or 130 per cent in 138 weeks, averaging 0.8 point per week. High speed at the end of

---

[17] Here Elliott correctly forecasts that one more new high will be made (which it was in late 1939) before the final bear market low (which occurred in 1942).

[18] This contention is not tenable, since every wave is itself both an "entire cycle" and a "component."

[19] This is another aspect of the Rule of Alternation.

long movements usually generates similar speed in the first wave of the reversal: compare the March 1938 downward movement with the following April reversal.

At certain stages volume seems to play an important part in the price movement, and volume itself will expand or contract to help control and complete the price cycle. Study of the time cycle and volume cycles is sometimes distinctly helpful in clarifying the position of the price spiral.[20] Volume tends to increase in the third wave of the cycle, and to maintain about the same activity in the fifth wave. As the bottom of the volume cycle is approached, erratic price changes in high priced stocks or inactive stocks with thin markets can distort the small waves in the trend of the averages to such an extent as to create temporary uncertainties. But these waves of volume are also useful in determining the extent and time for completion of price phases, and also in determining the time and direction and even the speed of the following movement. This is especially true in fast swinging markets like those that characterized 1938. The best results therefore will follow from correlation of the volume and time cycles with the component phases of the broad price movement, as the price patterns and all degrees of volume[21] are governed by precisely the same Wave Principle phenomenon.

To maintain a proper perspective, the student should chart at least two and preferably more broad averages, using the weekly range, the daily range, and the hourly record, and showing the accompanying volume. The weekly range should be sufficient properly to evaluate the broad changes in trend, but the monthly range studies will also undoubtedly appeal to many investors. The daily range, by affording close observation of the smaller changes, is essential in correct interpretation of the cyclical progression, and is quite necessary for determining the precise time of important reversals in trend.

---

[20] Here Elliott uses the word "spiral," reflecting the subjective feeling one gets while tracking waves. The theory of the logarithmic spiral as a model for the Wave Principle had not occurred to him.
[21] This is an assertion I have yet to investigate.

Critical Points

The minute changes recorded in the hourly study not only afford valuable and extensive material for practice in wave interpretation, but are especially useful in times when the market is moving at such high speed that the pattern is not clearly registered in the longer-time charts. Thus, the small triangle that appeared in the hourly record of October 1937 signalled an immediate acceleration or extension of the downward movement; the dynamic October 18-19 "panic" followed. At other critical points the hourly study has also proved valuable, as in locating the "orthodox top" before the final irregular top, thus selecting the time for strategic liquidation near the crest. As the first hourly phase following the break in March 1938 developed in five minute waves, it thus afforded a strong confirmation that the important trend had actually changed.

PART XII

Previous articles have discussed the theory of The Wave Principle and its application to broad market movements. The broader the category, the more clearly the wave impressions are outlined. The wave pattern of the comprehensive stock price averages such as the Dow Jones, The New York Times, or Standard Statistics averages, will correctly reflect the cyclical position of the market as a whole. Therefore, purchases and sales of a diversified list of representative stocks in accordance with the movements of the averages will result in profits, as their aggregate market value will swing in sympathy with the general market. But for the seeker of maximum profits consistent with safety, it is not enough to buy or sell a group of stocks without separate analysis of each individual stock.[22] These individual studies may reveal that some companies are experiencing a cycle differing greatly from that of the market as a whole. A prominent example was the case of American Can in the spring of 1935.

The accompanying charts depict the analysis of American Can[23] by The Wave Principle. In Figure 22 the complete monthly price range history is shown from June 1932 -- the beginning of the bull movement -- to June 1935, the time when the "orthodox top" occurred. The action of the stock from that point on to completion of the cyclical correction in December 1937 is shown in "trend lines." This monthly record condenses the weekly and daily details into the five broad Primary waves that

---

[22] Elliott's use of the Wave Principle to analyze stocks is somewhat selective. Many stocks do exhibit perfect wave qualities, but quite a few do not, since a single stock is not necessarily well representative of the mass psychological influence. It is probably very useful at times to ignore some of the rules of wave counting in order to discern the general effect of the Principle upon individual stocks, but such bending of the rules should only be done if absolutely necessary.

[23] In Figure 22, the correct count, avoiding overlapping and fulfilling third wave requirements, would be to place the ⒾⒾ where Elliott has an a, and (within wave ⒾⒾ) a 1 where he has a b, a 2 where he has a c, and a 3 where he has a 1. Wave 4 of ⒾⒾ then takes an a-b-c count, and the rule of alternation is still satisfied.

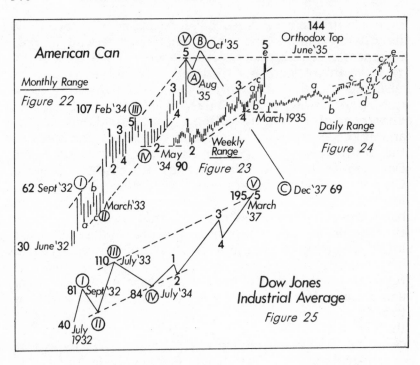

complete a cyclical movement. These relatively broad charts also help materially in maintaining the proper perspective.

When the important fifth Primary Wave of the cycle commenced in May 1934 -- or in other words, when the Primary Wave Ⓥ reaction was completed -- it became necessary to study the market action more closely. Hence Figure 23, which shows the weekly price record of the fifth Primary Wave. And after this Primary Wave had progressed through Intermediate Wave 4, it became important to follow the daily price ranges, as shown in Figure 24. The fifth Intermediate Wave started in March 1935, and five Minor waves were completed by June 1935. This signalled the "orthodox top"[24] of the main bull movement in American Can at 144.

Following the "orthodox top" of the bull cycle in American Can, there developed a reaction to 136-137 in August 1935, forming Wave Ⓐ. Then a rally to 149-150 in October 1935 forming Wave Ⓑ, the irregular but final top. From this point developed the long Wave Ⓒ in five Intermediate movements, terminating at 69 in December 1937.

At the time of the "orthodox top" in American Can, the investor would have observed the striking difference between the cyclical positions of that stock and of the general market. See Figure 25, which outlines the trend lines of the important Primary waves of the Dow-Jones Industrial Averages. In March 1935, American Can was in the final stages of a bull cycle (fifth Intermediate Wave of the fifth Primary). On the other hand the general market was just commencing the fifth Primary Wave, and still had to experience five upward Intermediate Waves. By June 1935, the long term investor in American Can would have realized that any further appreciation in that stock would be highly uncertain, and that much greater profits were available in the general market with minimum risks. From that point the general market advanced nearly 80 points or 65 per cent.

---

24 In Figure 24, Elliott ignores the overlapping and the insufficient third wave (labeled "c"). From the description of the supposed Ⓐ and Ⓑ waves that follow, it seems highly likely that the third wave of the final wave 5 of Ⓥ simply extended, thus eliminating the imperfect count. Elliott's a and b are all right, but his c could be reserved for the first peak within the supposed Ⓑ (thereby completing an extension from the low at b), the d for the next small reaction (the b of the Ⓑ), and the e for the actual high. It is evident that Elliott calls several tops "irregular" which might be better explained by extensions. The main reason for his opting for the "irregular top" in cases where it does not apply is his tendency to take patterns with third wave extensions and interpret them as if the fifth wave were extended, since he considered the fifth wave extension the most common.

NATURE'S LAW
THE SECRET OF THE UNIVERSE
by
R. N. ELLIOTT

REFERENCE INDICATIONS[1]

Reference to chapters, pages, diagrams, etc. will be indicated as follows:

(C)   Chapter. For example, "C 24" means Chapter No. 24.

(D)   Diagram. For example, "D 4" means diagram No. 4.

(FSS) Numbers of the Fibonacci Summation Series

(OT)   Orthodox top.

(G)   Graph. For example, "G X" means "Graph X".

(P)   Page. For example, "P 5" means Page 5.

(P D)   "P2 D4" means Page 2, Diagram 4.

(P G)   "P3 G6" means Page 3, Graph 6.

(P P D) "P4 P6 D8" means Page 4, Paragraph 6, Diagram 8.

(R)   Ruling ratio of the Fibonacci Summation Series, such as .62 or reciprocal 1.62.

PUBLISHER'S NOTE: In the original monograph, nearly every sentence was treated as a separate paragraph and numbered. We have taken the liberty of condensing the style of arrangement for easier reading. The references to text areas by codes as described above have been eliminated.

---

[1] Elliott's talent for ordering and labeling comes out even here.

NATURE'S LAW

THE SECRET OF THE UNIVERSE

By R. N. ELLIOTT

Vitally Important for

Traders in Securities, Commodities, etc.; Investors; Customers'
Brokers; Market Technicians; Bankers; Business Managers;
Economists; Trusts.

✦

Of Interest to

Artists, see page 9; Botanists, see pages 9, 51; Egyptologists, see
pages 7, 8, 51; Inventors, see pages 38, 39; Mathematicians, see
pages 7, 9, 29, 31, 51; Philosophers, see page 4; Physicians, see
page 55; Psychologists, see pages 7, 24; Pyramidists, see pages
7, 8, 29, 51, 59; Pythagoreans, see pages 7, 8, 56, 57, 58; Students of
Dynamic Symmetry, see pages 8, 9, 10, 11.

INTRODUCTION

RHYTHM IN NATURE[2]

No truth meets more general acceptance than that the universe is ruled by law. Without law it is self-evident there would be chaos, and where chaos is, nothing is. Navigation, chemistry, aeronautics, architecture, radio transmission, surgery, music -- the gamut, indeed, of art and science -- all work, in dealing with things animate and things inanimate, under law because nature herself works in this way. Since the very character of law is order, or constancy, it follows that all that happens will repeat and can be predicted if we know the law.

Columbus, maintaining that the world was round, predicted that a westward course from Europe must eventually bring his ships to land and despite scoffers, even among his own crew, saw his prediction realized. Halley, calculating the orbit of the 1682 comet, predicted its return which was strikingly verified in 1759. Marconi, after his studies in electrical transmission, predicted that sound could be conveyed without wires, and today we can sit in our homes and listen to musical and other programs from across the ocean. These men, as have countless more in other fields, learned the law. After becoming thus posted, prediction was easy because it became mathematical.

Even though we may not understand the cause underlying a particular phenomenon, we can, by observation, predict that phenomenon's recurrence. The sun was expected to recurrently rise at a fixed time thousands of years before the cause operating to produce this result was known. Indians fix their month by each new moon, but even today cannot tell why regular intervals characterize this heavenly sign. Spring plantings are witnessed the world over because summer is expected as next in order; yet how many planters understand why they are afforded this constancy of the seasons? In each instance the rhythm of the particular phenomenon was mastered.

---

[2] Except for minor revisions, this Introduction is the same as Chapter I of The Wave Principle.

Man is no less a natural object than the sun or the moon, and his actions, too, in their metrical occurrence, are subject to analysis. Human activities,while amazing in character, if approached from the rhythmical bias, contain a precise and natural answer to some of our most perplexing problems. Furthermore, because man is subject to rhythmical procedure, calculations having to do with his activites can be projected far into the future with a justification and certainty heretofore unattainable.

Very extensive research in connection with what may be termed human activities indicates that practically all developments which result from our social-economic processes follow a law that causes them to repeat themselves in similar and constantly recurring serials of waves or impulses of definite number and pattern. It is likewise indicated that in their intensity, these waves or impulses bear a consistent relation to one another and to the passage of time. In order to best illustrate and expound this phenomenon it is necessary to take, in the field of man's activities, some example which furnishes an abundance of reliable data and for such purpose there is nothing better than the stock exchange.

Particular attention has been given to the stock market for two reasons. In the first place, there is no other field in which prediction has been essayed with such great intensity and with so little result. Economists, statisticians, technicians, business leaders, and bankers all have had a try at foretelling the future of prices over the New York Stock Exchange. Indeed, there has developed a definite profession with market forecasting as its objective. Yet 1929 came and went and the turn from the greatest bull market on record to the greatest bear market on record caught almost every investor off guard. Leading investment institutions, spending hundreds of thousands of dollars yearly on market research, were caught by surprise and suffered millions of dollars loss because of price shrinkage in stock holdings that were carried too long.

A second reason for choosing the stock market as an illustration of the wave impulse common to social-economic activity is the great reward attendant on successful stock market prediction. Even accidental success in some single market forecast has yielded riches little short of the fabulous. In the market advance from July 1932 to March 1937, for illustration, an average of thirty leading and representative stocks advanced by 373%. During the course of this five-year movement, however, there were individual stocks whose per cent advance was much larger. Lastly, the broad advance cited above was not in a straight upward line, but rather by a series of upward and downward steps, or zig-zag movements of a number of months' duration. These lesser swings afforded even greater opportunity for profit.

Despite the attention given the stock market, success, both in the accuracy of prediction and the bounties attendant thereto, has necessarily been haphazard becasuse those who have attempted to deal with the market's movements have failed to recognize the extent to which the market is a psychological phenomenon. They have not grasped the fact that there is regularity underlying the fluctuations of the market, or, stated otherwise, that price movements in stocks are subject to rhythms, or an ordered sequence. Thus market predictions, as those who have had any experience in the subject well know, have lacked certainty or value of any but an accidental kind.

But the market has its law, just as is true of other things throughout the universe. Were there no law, there could be no center about which prices could revolve and, therefore, no market. Instead, there would be a daily series of disorganized, confused price fluctuations without reason or order anywhere apparent. A close study of the market, however, as will be subsequently disclosed, proves that this is not the case. Rhythm, or regular, measured, and harmonious movement, is to be discerned. This law behind the market can be discovered only when the market is viewed in its proper light, and then is analyzed from this approach. Simply put, the stock market is a creation of man and therefore reflects human idiosyncrasy. In the pages which follow, the law, or rhythm, to which man responds will be disclosed as registered by market movements that fluctuate in accordance with a definite wave principle.

Nature's Law has always functioned in every human activity. Waves of different degrees occur whether or not recording machinery is present. When the machinery described below is present, the patterns of waves are perfected and become visible to the experienced eye. This machinery is:

1. Extensive commercial activity represented by corporations whose ownership is widely distributed.

2. A general market-place where buyer and seller may contact quickly through representatives.

3. Reliable record and publications of transactions.

4. Adequate statistics available on all matters relating to corporations.

5. Daily high and low range charted in such a manner as will disclose the waves of all degrees as they occur.

The daily range of stock transactions was inaugurated in 1928 and the hourly record in 1932. These are necessary in order to observe the minor and minute waves, especially in fast markets.

Contrary to teachings of the Dow Theory, a popular device for guaging stock market movements, "Nature's Law" does not require confirmation by two averages. Each average, group, stock or any human activity is interpreted by its own waves.

CHAPTER I

THE GREAT PYRAMID GIZEH

Many years ago I endeavored to ascertain the meaning of the word "cycle" but no one could define it. Curiosity led to a study of graphs, and I discovered rhythm in fluctuations (as disclosed in my treatise published in 1938). Later I found that the basis of my discoveries was a law of Nature known to the designers of the Great Pyramid Gizeh which may have been constructed five thousand years ago.

There are several pyramids in Egypt and elsewhere but Gizeh is the original, and the only one that discloses symbols. Other pyramids were subsequently built to serve as crypts for the bodies of kings and their families. As early as 820 B.C. Al Mamoun, a Turkish Caliph, erroneously supposed that Gizeh housed the bodies of former pharaohs and that hoards of gold might be found. This proves that even at that early date the symbols of Gizeh were unknown. The period of Gizeh's construction was not only pre-literary but pre-hieroglyphic. Hieroglyphics are present in other pyramids but not in Gizeh.

Immense sums of money have been expended to learn the symbols of Gizeh, especially during the past fifty years. Their definitions are remarkably correct insofar as today's knowledge permits an understanding. Much of this knowledge is comparatively recent and indicates that the scientific symbols embodied in Gizeh must have been supernatural or that previous civilizations existed which equalled or exceeded today's development.[3] It is possible that a high degree of civilization previously existed on the Western Hemisphere, especially from Mexico to Argentina. The Bible mentions giants and quite recently jaws of giants have been found that may have weighed four or five hundred pounds.[4]

Insofar as I have been able to learn, Egyptologists overlooked certain important symbols contained in the Great Pyramid, such as the ratio of the elevation

[3] Such a civilization may have coincided with the last Millennium Cycle peak.
[4] Since proved to be otherwise, of course!

to the base of the pyramid which is 61.8% and the number of inches of the elevation which is 5,813. (Note the numbers 5, 8, and 13, mentioned below in the Summation Series.) The unit of measurement in Egypt was, and is, the "inch" as we know it today.

The outlines of a side view is that of a cycle, that is, 3 lines; in a pyramid there are 5 surfaces, four above ground and one at the bottom; from the apex 8 lines are visible; total surfaces and lines: 13.

Fibonacci, an Italian mathematician of the thirteenth century, visited Egypt and on his return disclosed a summation series as follows: 1 2 3 5 8 13 21 34 55 89 144.... Any two adjoining numbers equal the next higher -- for example, 5 + 8 = 13. The ratio of any number to the next higher is 61.8%. (The lower numbers produce a ratio slightly at variance). Therefore the elevation to the base of the pyramid provides a ratio that rules this entire series.

The seeds of a sunflower are located in curved rows that intersect each other. The highest number of intersections is 144. This is also the number of Minor waves in a complete cycle of the stock market (bull and bear markets). Numbers of the series are present in the human body, botany, production, animals, music and waves of human activities including the stock market.

Pythagoras, a Greek philosopher of the fifth century B. C., visited Egypt and on his return disclosed the diagram and title shown in Chapter 2.

CHAPTER II

NATURE'S LAW

Nature's Law was known at least five thousand years ago. Egypt was "in flower" at least 1,500 B. C. and is the oldest of today's list of nations. It is not known when the Egyptian pyramids were built. The Great Pyramid Gizeh was constructed at least five thousand years ago. Some students advance evidence that it existed before the threat of floods that prompted Noah to build the ark. Other students believe that it may be thirty thousand years old.

In Life magazine (December 3, 1945) there appears a very interesting article entitled "The Building of the Great Pyramid." Mr. Bel Geddes prepared models of different stages of construction and pictures of them are shown. The report was prepared for the Encyclopedia Brittanica. It says that the total weight of material used was 3,277,000 tons, whereas the material used in the Empire State Building, the tallest building in the world, weighs only 305,000 tons.

The marvelous ingenuity, skill, time and labor expended by the designers and builders of the pyramids to erect a perpetual symbol demonstrates the supreme importance of the messages they desired to convey to posterity. That era was pre-literary and pre-hieroglyphic, therefore symbols were the only means of recording.

For centuries the pyramids have been exhaustively investigated, especially during recent years. Insofar as I have observed, Egyptologists overlooked an important, perhaps the most important symbol. I refer to the outer lines of the pyramid Gizeh.

Pythagoras was a renowned Greek philosopher of the fifth century B. C. The older cyclopedias give a very detailed description of his activities. The Encyclopedia Brittanica shows a diagram and cryptic title which may be the only record he left. It was made after he returned to Greece following a prolonged visit to Egypt. The diagram and title appear in Figure 1. It is fair to assume that the Pythagoras diagram refers to a pyramid.

Figure 1

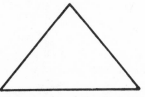

The Secret of the Universe

The original measurements of the Great Pyramid of Gizeh are estimated to have been: base 783.3 feet, elevation 484.4 feet, ratio 61.8%. The elevation, 484.4 feet, equals 5,813 inches (5-8-13 FSS).

Looking at a pyramid from any one of the four sides, 3 lines are visible. The diagram in Figure 2 is a complete cycle. Viewing the pyramid from any one of the four corners as in Figure 3, 5 lines are visible. A pyramid has 5 surfaces -- four above ground and the bottom. From the apex, a pyramid shows 8 lines, as shown in Figure 4.

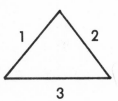

Figure 2

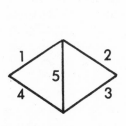

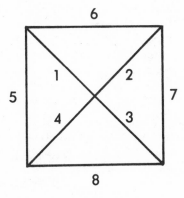

Figure 3   *Figure 4*

Fibonacci was an Italian mathematician of the thirteenth century, A. D. He was better known in his day as Leonardo de Piza. He visited Egypt and Greece and on his return to Italy disclosed what is known as a summation series. This series of numbers follows: 1 2 3 5 8 13 21 34 55 89 144....

Any two adjoining numbers equal the next higher number, for example, 5 + 8 = 13. Any number divided by the next higher number gives a ratio of .618, for example, 8/13 = .618. Any number divided by the next lower number gives a reciprocal of 1.618. In the lower numbers the ratios are not exact but close enough for practical purposes. To simplify reading I will hereafter refer to the former as .62 and the latter as 1.62.

Note that the first five numbers of the Summation Series, 1, 2, 3, 5, and 8, are shown in the complete diagram of a pyramid.

The late Jay Hambidge, an American artist, visited Egypt, Greece and Italy and wrote several very important and interesting books. By permission of Yale University Press, I quote pages 27 and 28 of his book entitled Practical Applications of Dynamic Symmetry:

Botanists use the disk of the sunflower as a sort of general illustration of the law of leaf arrangement. It exhibits the phenomenon in nearly two-dimensional form. The seeds are distributed over the sunflower disk in rhomboidal shaped sockets and the complex of these sockets forms a design of intersecting curves, the pattern being something like the old-fashioned chasing on watchcases. This pattern of curves is the interesting feature of the sunflower seed arrangement.

First. The curve itself is a definite kind of curve. As a matter of fact it is quite like the curve of shell growth. It is regular and possesses certain mathematical properties. Thes properties are a necessary consequence of uniform growth as will be explained presently.

Second. When these curves are counted it will be found that a normal sunflower disk of five or six inches in diameter has 89. Winding in one direction there are 55 and in the other direction there are 34. That is to say, the normal head exhibits 55 curves crossing 34. The two numbers are written 34 + 55. Below the apex flower of the stalk there are usually secondary flowers, smaller in size. The curve-crossing numbers for these are generally 21 + 34. Lower on the stalk may be tertiary flowers of late development. The curve-crossing numbers of these are 13 + 21.

At Oxford, in England, sunflowers have been nourished to produce abnormal disks and the curve-crossing numbers have increased from 34 + 55 to 55 + 89. Professor Arthur H. Church, a leading modern authority on this fascinating subject, tells us of a gigantic disk raised at Oxford whereon the curve-crossing numbers were 89 + 144.

Around the seed complex of the flower disk there is an arrangement of florets. Like the seeds, these exhibit curve-crossing numbers. They are usually 5 + 8.

If we begin at the bottom of the plant stalk and count the actual number of leaves up to the flower disk, we are likely to find, as we wind our progress around the stalk, that we pass a certain number of leaves before we find one imposed directly over the one first counted and that this number and the number of revolutions about the stalk, are constant between each leaf imposition. These will represent curve-crossing numbers belonging to the same series of numbers exhibited by the seeds and florets.

The numbers we have mentioned belong to what is called a summation series, so called because each number represents a sum of preceding numbers of the series, in this case 2. This series of numbers is: 1, 2, 3, 5, 8, 13, 21, 34, 55, 89, 144 etc. Each member of this series is obtained by adding together two preceding numbers.

If we take any two members of this series and divide one into the other as, say 34 into 55, we obtain a ratio, and this ratio is constant throughout the series; that is to say, any lesser number divided into any greater number which immediately succeeds it produces the same ratio. This ratio is 1.618 plus, a number with a never ending fraction. If we reverse the operation and divide 55 into 34 we obtain the number .618 plus. It will be noticed that the difference between these two results is 1 or unity.

It will also be noticed that when we make these two divisional operations that there is a slight error. This is due to the fact that the series is not quite accurate when expressed in whole numbers. There should be a very small fraction. But as the error is within that of observation in the growing plant, the whole number is retained to facilitate checking.

It is an extraordinary coincidence that this ratio of 1.618 or .618 is a ratio which fascinated the ancient Greeks exceedingly. Extraordinary, because they could have had no suspicion that it was connected with the architecture of plants. It was called by them "extreme" and "mean" ratio.

During the middle ages it was given the name Divine Section and in fairly recent time, Golden Section.

From experience I have learned that 144 is the highest number of practical value. In a complete cycle of the stock market, the number of Minor waves is 144, as shown in the following table and in Figure 7, Chapter 4:

Number of Waves	Bull Market	Bear Market	Total (complete cycle)
Major	5	3	8
Intermediate	21	13	34
Minor	89	55	144

All are Fibonacci numbers and the entire series is employed. The length of waves may vary but not the number. Note the FSS numbers in the following:

-- The bodies of humans follow the numbers 3 and 5. From the torso there are 5 projections -- head, two arms and two legs. Each leg and arm is subdivided into 3 sections. Legs and arms terminate in 5 toes and fingers. The toes and fingers (except the big toe) are subdivided into 3 sections. We have 5 senses.

-- The monkey is the same as a human except that

his feet are the same as his hands, that is, his big toe is the same as his thumb. Most animals have 5 projections from the torso -- head and four legs, total 5. Birds have 5 projections from the torso -- head, two feet and two wings.

-- Music: The best example is the piano keyboard. "Octave" means eight. Each octave is composed of 8 white keys and 5 black keys, total 13.

-- Chemical elements: There are approximately 89 primary elements.

-- Colors: There are 3 primary colors. Blending produces all other colors.

Miscellaneous Observations:[5]

-- The Western Hemisphere is composed of 3 sub-divisions, North, Central and South America.

-- In the Western Hemisphere there are 21 Republics, all of which are members of the Pan-American Union. North America is composed of 3 countries, Canada, Mexico and the United States. South America is composed of ten Republics and three European colonies, total 13. Central America was, previous to the Panama Canal, composed of 5 Republics.

-- The United States was originally composed of 13 states. Today there are 55 subdivisions as follows: forty-eight states, District of Columbia, Philippines, Panama Canal Zone, Puerto Rico, Alaska, Hawaiian Islands and the Virgin Islands.

-- On the Declaration of Independence there are 56 signatures. The original number was 55. The last was added later.

---

[5] While the Fibonacci numbers have significance in his primary examples, these "miscellaneous observations," while interesting, appear to be an excercise in numerology.

-- Main branches of the Federal Government: 3.
-- Highest salute of the Army: 21 guns.
-- Voting age: 21 years.
-- The Bill of Rights contains: 13 points.
-- The colors of the national flag are: 3.

-- The Washington Monument in Washington, D. C. (The cornerstone was laid July 4, 1848.):

Total cost, $1,300,000.	13
Height of shaft, 500 feet.	5
Height of capstone, 55 feet.	55
Base of shaft, 55 feet square.	55
Top rim of shaft, 34 feet.	34
Steps of foundation (number):	8
Windows (two on each side):	8

The capstone is in the form of a pyramid with a base 34 feet square and a height 55 feet (ratio .618).

-- The Axis was composed of 3 partners. Germany dominated 13 countries in rapid succession but stalled on the fourteenth, Russia. Mussolini served as dictator for 21 years.

-- In 1852 Commodore Perry paid a courtesy visit to Japan and invited the "Son of Heaven" to abandon absolute isolationism. In 1907, 55 years later, Japan seriously threatened the United States. In 1941, 34 years later, and 89 years from 1852, Japan attacked Pearl Harbor.

CHAPTER III

HUMAN ACTIVITIES

The expression "human activities"[6] includes such items as stock prices, bond prices, patents, price of gold, population, movements of citizens from cities to farms and vice versa, commodities prices, government expenditures, production, life insurance, electric power produced, gasoline consumption, fire losses, price of seats on the stock exchange, epidemics, and real estate. The main item of interest is the price of securities, which everyone should understand at least to some degree.

It behooves us to prepare for the "rainy day." Permanent improvements, such as the construction of buildings, conservation projects, roads, bridges, factories, homes, etc. should await cyclical lows for the double purpose of low cost to the owner and the employment of labor. Fluctuations in economic welfare are as unfailing as the earth's revolution.

---

[6] See the charts in the final pages of The Wave Principle.

CHAPTER IV

DISTINCTIVE FEATURES OF HUMAN ACIVITIES

All human activities have three distinctive features -- pattern, time and ratio -- all of which observe the Fibonacci Summation Series. Once the waves can be intrepreted, the knowledge may be applied to any movement, as the same rules apply to the price of stocks, bonds, grains, cotton, coffee and all the other activities previously mentioned.

The most important of the three factors is pattern. A pattern is always in process of formation. Usually, but not invariably, the student is able to visualize in advance the type of pattern. This facility is furnished by the type of pattern that preceded. See Chapter 8, "Alternation."

A perfect diagram of a stock market cycle is shown in Figures 5, 6 and 7. It is divided primarily into "bull market" and "bear market." Figure 5 subdivides the bull market into five Major[7] waves and the bear market into three Major waves. The diagram of the bull market in Figure 6 subdivides Major waves ①, ③ and ⑤[8] into five Intermediate waves each. Figure 7 subdivides Intermediate waves 1, 3 and 5 into five Minor waves each.

In Figure 5, the bear market is subdivided into three Major waves indicated by the letters Ⓐ, Ⓑ and Ⓒ. In Figure 6, downward waves Ⓐ and Ⓒ are subdivided into five Intermediate waves. Wave Ⓑ upward is divided into three Intermediate waves. In Figure 7, the Intermediate waves are subdivided into Minor waves.

In other words, a bear market is the reverse of a bull market, except that a bear market has three Major waves down, whereas in a bull market there are five Major waves upward. Corrections in both bull and bear swings are more difficult to learn.

---

[7] The term "Major" is used throughout the next several chapters as a substitute for the term "Primary," which was introduced in the first monograph.

[8] Elliott has altered the wave labels developed in the first monograph, probably because the original numbering was somewhat cumbersome.

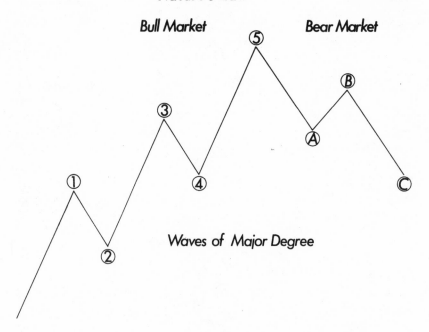

Figure 5

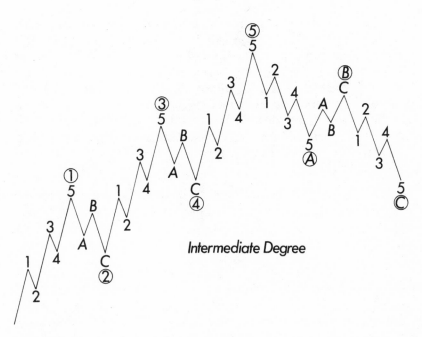

Figure 6

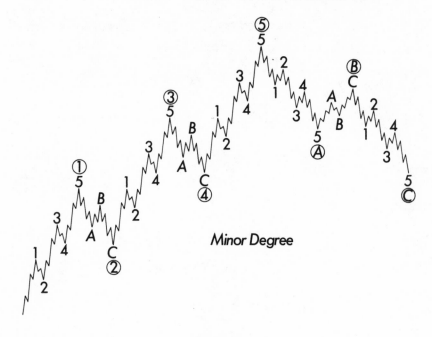

Figure 7

As the discoveries disclosed herein are original, new expressions had to be coined. In order to explain the patterns and their corresponding expressions, perfect diagrams are shown in various degrees. The word "degree" means relative importance, so to speak. For example, "Major" degree refers to those waves in Figure 5. "Intermediate" degree refers to waves in Figure 6. "Minor" degree refers to waves shown in Figure 7. See Chapter 2 for numbers of waves.

CHAPTER V

CORRECTIONS

Patterns of corrections are the same, regardless of their direction or size. In a bull swing, corrections are downward or sidewise. In a bear swing corrections are upward or sidewise. Therefore, corrections will be diagramed for both bull and bear swings. The diagrams first shown apply to upward swings. Diagrams underneath apply to downswings and will be "inverted." Therefore, whenever the expression "inverted" appears, it applies to the downward main trend.

In Figures 5, 6 and 7 it will be noted that there are three degrees of waves: Major, Intermediate and Minor. Likewise there are three degrees of corrections, as is natural.[9]

There are three types of corrections: Zigzag, Flat and Triangle.

Zigzags

Figures 8, 9 and 10 are corrections of an uptrend.

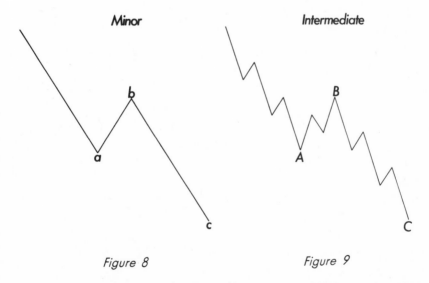

Figure 8   Figure 9

---

[9] Figures 10 and 13 are actually drawings of "double zigzags," which Elliott displays in Chapter 6. Either Elliott mis-drew his illustrations here or he decided that double zigzags were more common in Major degree than

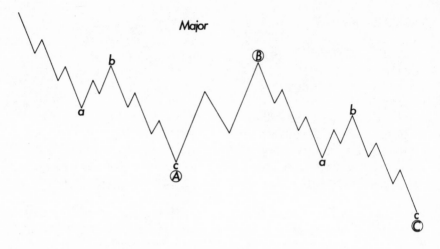

Figure 10

Figures 11, 12 and 13 are inverted (corrections of a downtrend).

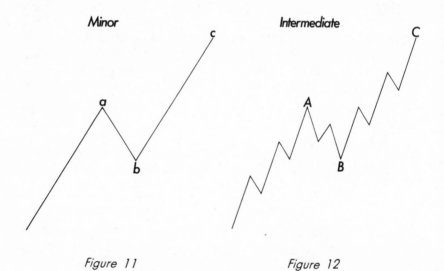

Figure 11   *Figure 12*

regular zigzags. For an illustration of a true zigzag of Major degree, refer to the Ⓐ-Ⓑ-Ⓒ section of Figure 7, as well as Figure 15 in the Financial World articles and Figure 27 in The Wave Principle.

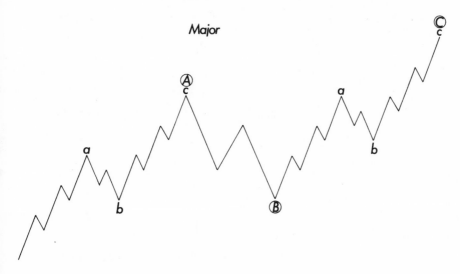

Figure 13

Flats

The next illustrations are flats of Minor, Intermediate and Major degree, both ordinary (Figures 14, 15 and 16) and inverted (Figures 17, 18 and 19). These diagrams are given the name "flat" for the reason that their usual appearance is flat. At times, they slant downward or upward.

As a matter of fact, these patterns might be called "3-3-5." In the last analysis they are three wave patterns, i.e., A, B and C, whereas a bull pattern is a "5-3-5-3-5" for waves 1, 2, 3, 4 and 5.

The pattern of a human being is "5-3-5-3." There are 5 projections from the torso (head, two arms and two legs); the arms and legs are subdivided into 3 sections; the ends of arms and legs are subdivided into 5 fingers or 5 toes; each finger and toe is again subdivided into 3 sections.

Whether or not Wave C of an inverted flat is elongated, it still remains corrective. It is possible, however, to know when an elongated wave C will occur by reading carefully Chapter 8, "Alternation."

Minor

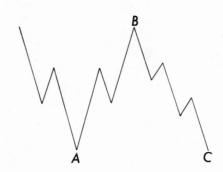

Figure 14

Intermediate

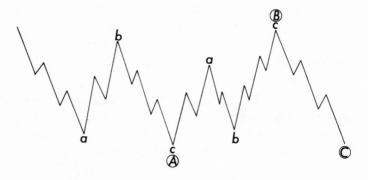

Figure 15

Major

Figure 16

Minor

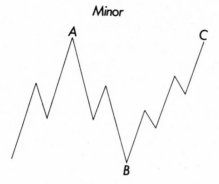

Figure 17

Intermediate

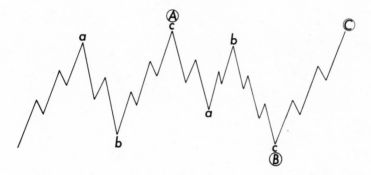

Figure 18

Major

Figure 19

Complex Corrections

A minor correction would be composed of three waves down, as in Figures 20 and 21.

Figure 20   Figure 21

A double sidewise correction would be composed of seven waves as in Figure 22. A triple sidewise movement would have eleven waves as in Figure 23.

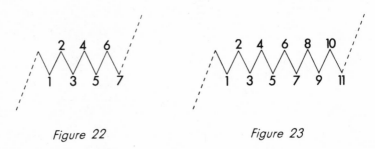

Figure 22   Figure 23

In other words, a sidewise correction to an uptrend always ends in a down wave[10], whether it is composed of one, three, seven or eleven waves. They are named as follows: three waves is a "single three," seven waves is a "double three" and eleven waves is a "triple three."

The same number of waves upward are corrective, as in Figures 24, 25 and 26.

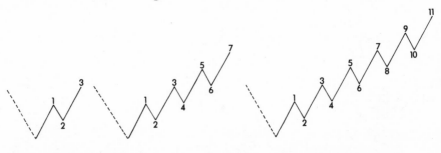

Figure 24   Figure 25   Figure 26

Occasionally these threes are mixed in upward and sidewise, or downward and sidewise, as in Figures 27 and 28 (double threes mixed),[11] and 29 and 30 (double threes upward).

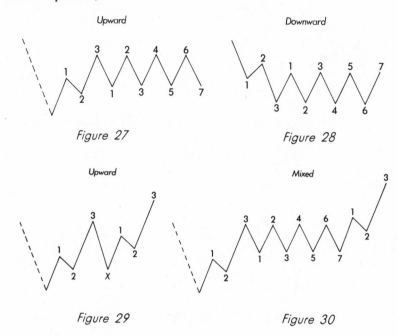

Figure 27   Figure 28

Figure 29   Figure 30

Triangles

Triangles are composed of five waves, or better said, five legs. In the larger types, each leg will be composed of three waves each as shown in Figures 31 and 32.

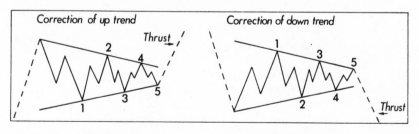

Figure 31   Figure 32

[10] Elliott overlooked this statement when drawing the illustrations in Figures 27 and 28, which cannot serve to reinstate the trends previously in motion.

[11] Elliott inadvertently left out an additional "three" in each of Figures 27 and 28.

In medium sized types, the fourth and fifth legs may be composed of one wave each, as in Figure 33. In the very small types the legs are often composed of just one wave. The main guide to the formation of a triangle is the outline, that is, the straight lines drawn across the tops and bottoms. The student cannot be certain that a triangle is forming until the fifth wave has started.

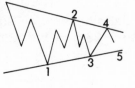

Figure 33

There are three types of triangles, shown in Figure 34.

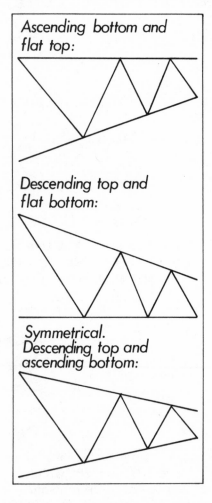

Figure 34

The fifth leg may terminate within or without the outline of the triangle, as in Figures 35 and 36.

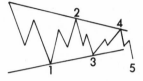

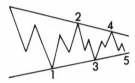

Figure 35   *Figure 36*

The fifth wave should be composed of three waves unless the triangle is very small. On one occasion a triangle consumed only seven hours. The largest triangle occurred between November 1928 and April 1942, thirteen years.[12] This latter movement will be discussed in other chapters.

The movement subsequent to the fifth leg of a triangle is called a "thrust." It will be composed of five waves and be in the direction of legs 2 and 4 of the triangle.

Triangles are infrequent. When they appear, their position has always been wave 4 of a movement of any degree, up or down, as shown in Figures 37 and 38.

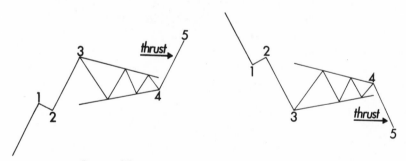

Figure 37   *Figure 38*

The fifth wave, which follows a triangle, is called a "thrust" and is composed of five waves similar to those of waves 1 and 3. As shown above, the fifth wave exceeds the top of wave 3, as in Figure 37, or the bottom of wave 3, as in Figure 38.

---

[12] The thirteen-year triangle concept has been discarded by most wave analysts. See Footnotes 25-32.

CHAPTER VI

EXTENSIONS

An extension may appear in any one of the three impulses, i.e., waves 1, 3 or 5, but never in <u>more</u> than one, as shown in Figures 39, 40 and 41 (upward) and Figures 42, 43 and 44 (inverted).

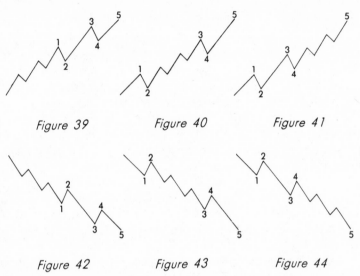

Figure 39   Figure 40   Figure 41

Figure 42   Figure 43   Figure 44

It will be noted that in each instance there are a total of nine waves, counting the extended wave as five instead of one. On rare occasions an extended movement will be composed of nine waves, all of equal size, as illustrated in Figures 45 and 46.

Figure 45   Figure 46

Extensions occur only in new territory of the current cycle. That is, they do not occur as corrections.

Extensions of Extensions

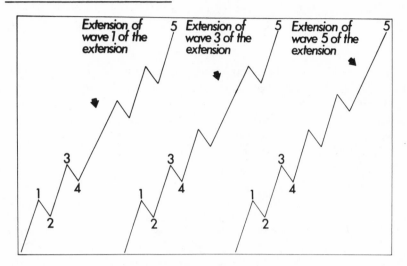

Figure 47

Extension in Wave 5 and Double Retracement

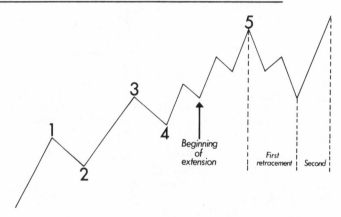

Figure 48

Extensions are "double retraced," that is, a correction will pass over the same ground twice, down and up. It is not necessary to give any consideration to this feature when the extension occurs in the first or third wave, but only when the extension occurs in the fifth wave. If the extension occurs in the first wave, the double retracement will be taken care of automatically[13] by waves 2 and 3. If the extension occurs in the third wave, double retracement will be taken care of by waves 4 and 5. See figure 48 for illustration of an extension in wave 5 and the subsequent double retracement.

If an extension is of small degree, retracement will occur immediately. But if it is of Intermediate or Major degree, double retracement may not occur until the entire advance has been completed.[14] When a movement occurs at high speed, the same territory is retraced at almost the same speed in reverse.

Erroneous Counting

The three impulse waves, 1, 3 and 5, are seldom of the same length. One of the three is usually considerably longer than either of the other two. It is important to note that wave 3 is never shorter than both waves 1 and 5. For example, when wave 3 is shorter than either[15] wave 1 or 5, as in Figure 49, the correct method of counting is as in Figure 50.

Note that wave 4 overlapped wave 1, which it should not do. Overlapping means that the end of wave 4 was lower than the top of wave 1. Inverted, the example would appear as in Figures 51 and 52.

---

[13] Certainly part of an extension in the first or third wave will be retraced, but it will not be retraced in the same manner as those within fifth waves. Only after fifth waves will the first retracement return as far back as the low of wave two of the extension.

[14] Based on Elliott's interpretation of the 1921-1928 advance, which he illustrates fully in Chapter 11, the double retracement of the fifth wave extension was not completed until after the first A-B-C irregular correction had taken place. The C wave of that correction was the 1929-1932 "crash," and due to the fact that the A wave was extremely small, only the first retracement was completed at the end of C, with both the orthodox top and irregular top already completed. The second retracement was completed with subsequent market action.

[15] A misstatement. He means, as he said before, "shorter than both waves 1 and 5." That is to say, wave 3 cannot be the shortest wave if one is counting correctly.

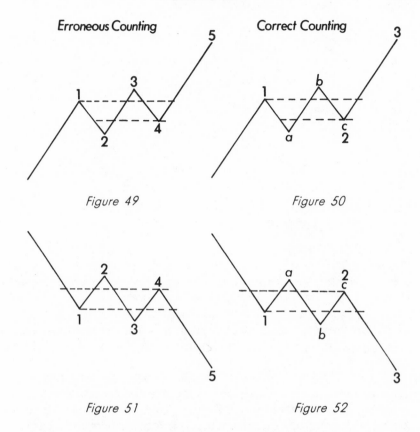

Figure 49

Figure 50

Figure 51

Figure 52

Overlapping within "complex" waves merits careful study. Occasionally complex waves develop into "double threes" or "triple threes," as diagrammed in Chapter 5.

Enlargement of Corrections

It is important to graph a movement in the daily range in order to know whether or not the first upward movement is composed of three or five waves. The weekly range might not disclose this fact. For example, in Figures 53 and 54, an inverted flat is shown in both daily and weekly range.[16] Note that in the weekly range the precise composition of the first wave up is not

---

[16] While these formations do come under the broad heading "flats," denoting 3-3-5 patterns, this type is more specifically referred to as "irregular" in the first monograph.

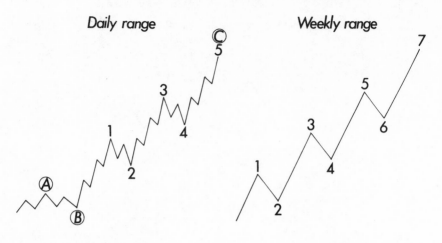

Figure 53   Figure 54

disclosed and the student might erroneously assume that it was composed of five waves in the daily. The weekly range of an inverted flat would appear as being composed of seven waves, whereas it would be an inverted flat, i.e., A, B, (1, 2, 3, 4, 5) C, as shown in Figure 53.

Similar behavior may occur in zigzags. A zigzag does not elongate but it may enlarge or double, so to speak, as illustrated in Figures 56 and 57. Whether a zigzag is single or double, its corrective character remains the same.

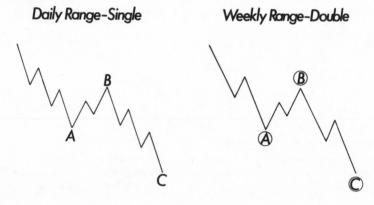

Figure 55   Figure 56

Sidewise Movements

As will have been noted, all corrective

Daily Range-Double

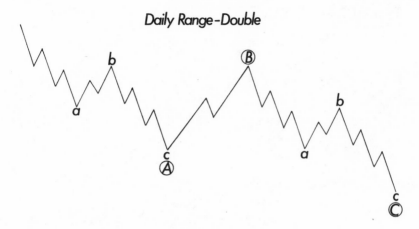

Figure 57

movements regardless of the degree are composed of three waves. Sidewise movements follow the same behavior, and are of the same character, corrective. Figure 58 shows two types of sidewise movements[17] following an advance. In Figure 59, the main trend is downward.

Main Trend Upward

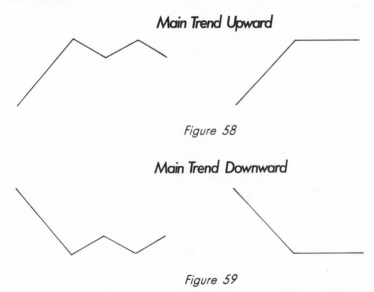

Figure 58

Main Trend Downward

Figure 59

[17] The first illustration in each of Figures 58 and 59 is a flat. The second merely shows the look of any flat correction of extremely small degree.

CHAPTER VII

IRREGULAR TOPS

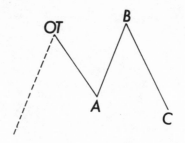

Figure 60

A movement that exceeds the top of a fifth wave (the orthodox top) is an "irregular" top. Suppose that the five waves up in Figure 61 are of Major degree. The top of the fifth wave would be the "orthodox" top (OT). The first movement from point "5" down would be composed of three waves and lettered "A." The second movement would be upward and exceed the top of 5. This movement would be lettered "B." Like wave A, it would be composed of three waves. The next movement would be composed of five waves down and lettered "C."

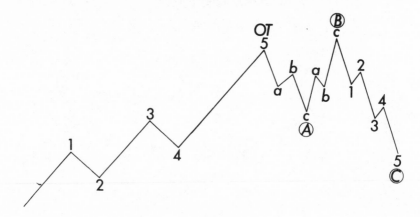

Figure 61

Waves A, B and C all constitute <u>one</u> correction, notwithstanding the fact that the end of wave B may be higher than wave 5. This occurred between November 1928 and July 1932.[18] A perfect understanding of this feature is important.

If wave A is a simple zigzag, wave B will be an inverted flat. This is a case where the law of Alternation gives a warning. "Alternation" is the subject of the next chapter.

---

¹⁸ See Footnote #17 in <u>The Wave Principle</u>.

CHAPTER VIII

ALTERNATION

According to the dictionary, alternation is "occurrence or action of two things or series of things, in turn." Alternation is a law of Nature. For instance, leaves or branches usually appear first on one side of the main stem and then of the opposite side, alternating their position. The composition of the human body follows the same rule: 5-3-5-3. An endless list of examples could be cited but the object of this discussion is the habit of alternation in human activity.

Bull and bear markets alternate. A bull market is composed of five waves and a bear market of three waves. Thus five and three alternate. The same rule governs in all degrees.

A bull movement is composed of five waves. Waves 1, 3 and 5 are upward. Waves 2 and 4 are downward or sidewise. Thus the odd numbers alternate with even numbers.

Waves 2 and 4 are corrective. These two waves alternate in pattern. If wave 2 is "simple," wave 4 will be "complex," and vice versa. A "simple" correction in the smaller degrees is composed of one wave downward. The "complex" is composed of three waves downward or sidewise. See Figures 62 and 63.

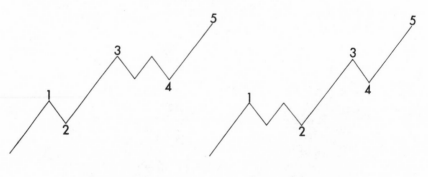

Figure 62   Figure 63

In the larger degrees, such as complete bull and bear markets, the corrective waves are correspondingly larger. Preparation for the final downswing is often tedious. First there is a downward movement of some importance which I letter with a capital A. This is followed by an upward swing and designated as wave B. The third and last movement downward is wave C. Wave A may be a zigzag pattern. In this event, wave B will be a flat, inverted. If wave A is a flat, wave B will be a zigzag, inverted. (In any event, wave C will be composed of five waves down. It may be severe and approach the starting point of the previous bull market.) Thus waves A and B alternate.

The thirteen-year triangle furnishes another example of alternation. From November 1928 to March 31, 1938 is a flat.[19] From March 31, 1938 to October 1939 is a zigzag, inverted. From October 1939 to May 1942 is a flat.[20]

An irregular top is one in which wave B exceeds the top of the fifth wave of the previous bull market, as explained in Chapter 7. Even these alternate. The top of 1916 was irregular, 1919 regular, 1929 irregular, 1937 regular.

Up to 1906 the Rails led upward movements. For 34 (FSS) years, from 1906 to 1940, the Industrials led upward movements. Since 1940 the Rails have been leading.

---

[19] See Footnotes #28 and #29.
[20] Actually, this is a "five," constituting wave C of the A-B-C from 1937.

CHAPTER IX

SCALES

To employ either semi-logarithmic or arithmetic scale and not the other as a general practice is erroneous, and deprives the student of their value and utility. The arithmetic scale should be employed unless and until log scale is demanded.

In a movement of five waves upward, a "base line" is drawn against the ends of waves 2 and 4, then a "parallel line" against the end of wave 3. Figure 64 shows the example.

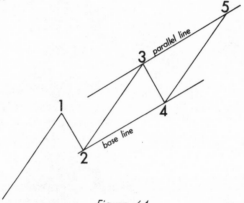

Figure 64

Usually wave 5 will end approximately at the parallel line when arithmetic scale is used. However, if wave 5 exceeds the parallel line considerably, and the composition of wave 5 indicates that it has not completed its pattern, then the entire movement from the beginning of wave 1 should be graphed on semi-log scale. The end of wave 5 may reach, but not exceed the parallel line. For example, if the same figures were graphed on both scales, the pictures would appear as in Figures 65 and 66.

When semi-log scale becomes necessary, inflation is present.[21] If semi-log scale is used and inflation is not present, wave 5 will fail to reach the parallel line by a good margin, as illustrated in Figure 67.

---

[21] "Inflation" as defined by Elliott in Chapter 12 is not monetary inflation as we know the term (see Footnote #33). Actually, the deciding factor in arithmetic vs. semi-log channeling is the shape of the wave. If

Arithmetic Scale

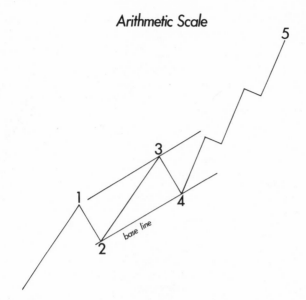

Figure 65

Log Scale

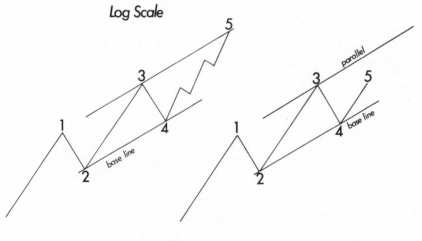

Figure 66   Figure 67

---

arithmetic scale is correct, then the move is developing with reference to points advanced. If semi-log scale is correct, the move is developing with reference to percentage advanced. Anyone can be given the same starting point and ending point and a specific time frame and draw a perfect Elliott wave on both arithmetic and semi-log scale.

EXAMPLES

Demonstrations of Nature's Law in previous pages have been made to facilitate an understanding of the graphs that follow.[22]

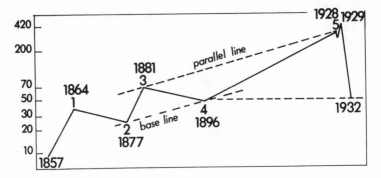

Figure 68

Figure 68 is an outline of the Axe-Houghton-Burgess Index from 1857 to 1932, drawn on semi-logarithmic scale. This is the largest degree for which records are available. Note the five waves from 1857 to November 1928. Note the base line drawn against waves 2 and 4 and the parallel line drawn against wave 3. The end of wave 5 touches the parallel line in November 1928.

The movement, as a whole, was inflationary; therefore semi-log is essential. However, arithmetic scale is essential when graphing the several bull markets individually.

Note that the decline to 1932 just reached the beginning of wave 5 in 1896. It was at this 1896 low point that the decline from 1929 to 1932 stopped -- in other words, a normal correction. Lack of knowledge of past history is the cause of the erroneous use of the expression "The Great Depression" and therefore emphasizes the vital importance of history, in this as well as all other activities.

---

[22] See Figure 98 in the final pages of the book for a look at the Grand Supercycle.

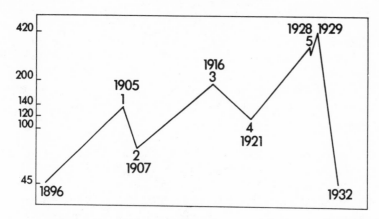

Figure 69

Figure 69 is a detail of wave 5 of Figure 68, drawn on semi-log scale. It is divided into five waves of the next lower degree.

Figure 70 is a graph of the Dow-Jones Industrials for the period 1921 to 1928, drawn on semi-log scale. Note the base line drawn against waves 2 and 4 and the parallel line drawn against wave 3, and that wave 5 just touches same.

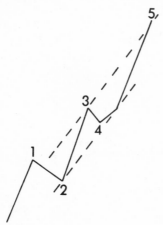

Figure 70

The movement from 1857 to November 1928 is composed of five waves as shown in Figure 68. The fifth wave from 1896 is subdivided into five waves, as shown in Figure 69. The fifth wave of this movement, starting from 1921, is again subdivided into five waves, as shown in Figure 70. In other words, the entire movement from 1857 is subdivided three times.

In Figure 71, the Dow-Jones Industrial Average is drawn on arithmetic scale, and again[23] the amplitude of waves 1 and 3 is 62% of wave 5.

From 1857 to 1928 there were seven bull markets and six bear markets, total 13 (FSS).[24] All bull markets from 1857 to 1928 were normal in extent. Remember that from 1921 to 1928 there were three bull markets and two bear markets, not one bull market. The two bear markets were sub-normal.

The time factor is important because it usually confirms and conforms to the pattern. For example, from 1928 to 1942 is 13 (FSS) years. From 1937 to 1942, 5 (FSS) years. Both periods end simultaneously. The entire movement from 1928 to 1942 is one pattern, a triangle. Each wave of the triangle is 62% of its predecessor. All three factors -- pattern, time and ratio -- are perfect, and in accordance with the Fibonacci Summation Series. See Figure 71.

In the previous pages Nature's Law has been explained. The numbers of the FSS apply in three ways: number of waves, time (number of days, weeks, months or years), and ratio of the FSS numbers, 62%.

---

[23] "Again," meaning as in the 1896-1928 advance shown in Figure 69 and the 1932-1937 advance shown in Figure 72.

[24] Apparently Elliott is counting the first wave up as one bull market and the third and fifth waves up as three bull markets each.

CHAPTER XI

THE THIRTEEN YEAR TRIANGLE[25]

The orthodox top of November 1928 is 299; the bottom of 1932 is 40; net travel: 259 points. The travel from 1932 to 1937 is from 40 to 195, net 155 points. The ratio of 155 to 259 is 60%.

From the orthodox top of November 1928 to July 1932 is wave ① of the thirteen-year triangle. From July 1932 to March 1937 is wave ② of the triangle, as shown in Figure 71. From March 1937 to March 1938 is wave ③ of the triangle.

---

[25] Elliott's troubles with interpretation in this volume are due almost entirely to the concept of the thirteen-year triangle. While many of the features in the 1928-1942 period are fascinating, and while the concept helped Elliott call a major low in 1942, the thirteen-year triangle concept as such is quite likely invalid. The main problems are that the 1932-1937 rise is a "five," the 1937-1938 decline is a "five," and the 1939-1942 decline is a "five," thus eliminating them as possible triangle legs since all triangle legs must be "threes." The most persuasive argument that a triangle had formed was the series of .618 retracements all within perfectly converging trend-lines, an occurrence which was indeed quite uncanny. However, this phenomenon can occur across different waves (as it did from 1976 to 1979), and is not enough justification, by itself, to claim that a true triangle is indeed being formed. Unfortunately, Elliott had made up his mind on an irrelevant point outside the Wave Principle, namely that 1929-1932 was too short a time period to correct the previous Supercycle. This assumption led him to the thirteen-year triangle interpretation, which in turn led him into trouble with his basics of the Wave Principle, as he tried to fit the subwaves into his predetermined concept. The 1929-1932 decline and the 1932-1937 advance were so clear that in effect they should have answered the question of time as follows: when a crash like 1929-1932 occurs, it's enough by itself to correct an entire Supercycle. Period. My reservations concerning this interpretation are expressed in the interests of clarifying the theory, and should not detract from the reader's enjoyment of Elliott's fascinating discoveries and analysis with regard to the period after the 1929 peak.

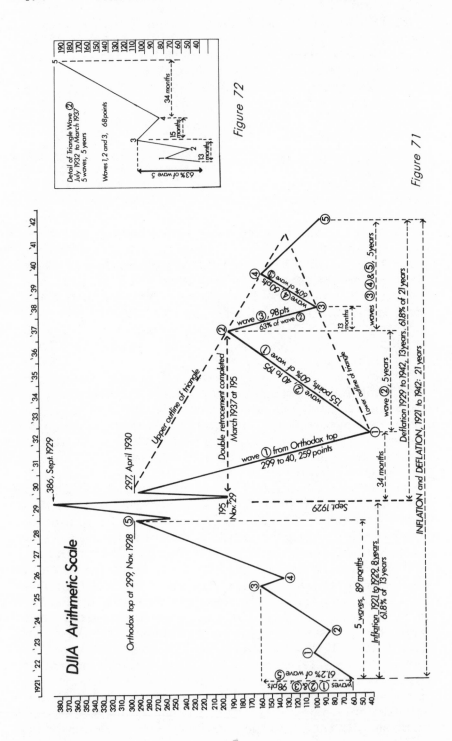

Figure 72

Figure 71

This index moved to 195 in March 1937 for reasons other than pattern, ratio and time. The advance from 1921 to 1928 was an extension of the fifth wave starting in 1896. As shown in Chapter 6, an extension is "double retraced." The decline to 195, from September to November, 1929 was part of the first retracement. The advance from 40 to 195 during 1932 to 1937 completed the double retracement.[26] Note the precise meeting at 195 of November 1929 and March 1937 in Figure 71.

It should be emphasized that the amplitude of the movement from 1932 to 1937 of 155 points is not that of a typical bull market.[27] Its extent was forced by the three powerful technical forced described above, i.e.,

-- The necessity of recovering 62% of the down movement from November 1928 at 299 to July 1932 at 40.
-- To complete double retracement of the 1921-1928 extension.
-- The time element, sixty months or 5 years.
-- Pattern.

------

[26] While these turning points are not coincidence, tying them to the "double retracement" rule, at least as it is stated in theory, seems to be stretching the rule a bit too far. The extension within the fifth wave of the 1921-1928 rise was doubly retraced, as necessary, the top part by Elliott's A and B, and the rest by 1 of C and 2 of C. The reason that the entire 1921-1928 rise failed to doubly retrace entirely by means of an irregular correction is that, as Frost and I have concluded, 1921-1929 was not itself an extended wave. Our data, which is based on constant-dollar prices, shows quite clearly that the extended wave in the 1857- 1929 sequence was the third, as is normal. Therefore the fifth would have no reason to be doubly retraced by an irregular top. The fact that the first retracement covered more than the entire fifth wave is further evidence that the wave was not an extension. Even if we consider it an extension, the ensuing fifth Supercycle wave would constitute the second retracement eventually as the rules allow. Still, the action of the market after the 1929 peak is quite intriguing and one can see why Elliott considered his double retracement rule satisfied.
[27] True. This is the most dramatic bull market in U. S. history in terms of percentage increase over time.

In fact, the movement complied with four requisites -- wave pattern, amplitude, double retracement and time -- all of which are based solely on FSS.

The ratio of amplitude of the 1921-1928 period is such that the advance of waves ① and ③ traveled 98 points, or 62% of wave ⑤, 160 points.

Note the horizontal lines across the bottom of Figures 71 and 72:

-- 1921 (beginning of inflation) to 1942 (end of deflation): 21 years.
-- 1921 to 1929: 8 years (62% of 13 years).
-- July 1921 to November 1928: 89 months.
-- September 1929 to July 1932: 34 months.
-- July 1932 to July 1933: 13 months.
-- July 1933 to July 1934: 13 months.
-- July 1934 to March 1937: 34 months.
-- July 1932 to March 1937: 5 years.
-- March 1937 to March 1938: 13 months.
-- March 1937 to April 1942: 5 years.
-- 1929 to 1942: 13 years (62% of 21 years).

The pattern and description of triangles are shown in Chapter 5. The triangle between November 1928 (the orthodox top) and April 1942 is the symmetrical type. It differs from the ordinary type because it is composed of two patterns, flat and zigzag. First there was a flat, then a zigzag and again a flat.[28] This was necessary because of its immense size, the alternation of patterns, the necessity of advancing to 195 in 1937 in order to complete a double retracement of the inflationary extension from 1921 to 1928, the necessity of completing its pattern by 1942 (21 years from 1921), the necessity of maintaining the ratio of 62%, and the necessity of retracing the entire fifth wave from 1896 to 1928, all of which is a very large order.

---

[28] The rule of alternation usually does apply to triangles, but it applies for each of the five subwaves in succession. Elliott is describing all of the first three waves together as a flat because the third wave of the triangle is so undeniably a "five."

The thirteen-year triangle from 1928 to 1942 was composed of three patterns, as follows:

-- November 1928 to March 1938: a flat[29] (triangle waves ①, ②, and ③).
-- March 1938 to October 1939: a zigzag, inverted (triangle wave ④).
-- October 1939 to April 1942: a flat (triangle wave ⑤).

Note the alternation of patterns: flat, zigzag and flat. Many other examples of similar nature could be cited. Both the flat and the inverted zigzag are described in Chapter 5. They and the corresponding triangle wave are reproduced in Figure 73.

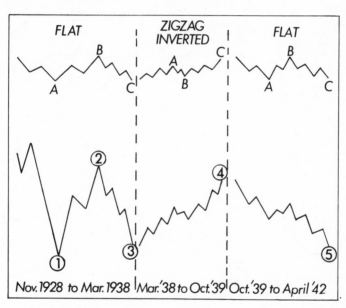

Figure 73

Figure 74 is a graph on arithmetic scale of the Dow-Jones Industrial Average from November 1928 to April 1942. Each vertical line represents the monthly range.

---

[29] Elliott breaks his own rules in this interpretation. If 1937-1938 is the "C" leg of a flat, it must be a "five." If it is a leg of his triangle, it must be a "three." He shouldn't be able to have it both ways.

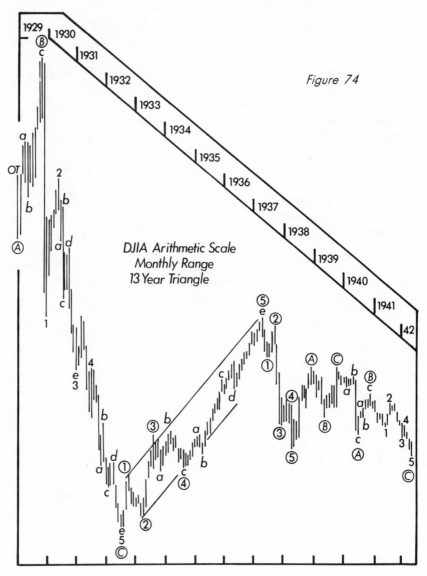

Figure 74

DJIA Arithmetic Scale
Monthly Range
13 Year Triangle

Triangle wave ① from 1928 to 1932 is composed of waves Ⓐ, Ⓑ and Ⓒ. Wave Ⓐ is composed of three waves down from November to December, 1928. They were fast and therefore visible only in the daily range. Wave Ⓑ is an irregular top in the form of an inverted flat. Wave Ⓒ is composed of five waves down from September 1929 to July 1932 (see numbers on chart), and consumed 34 months.

Triangle wave ② from 1932 to 1937 is a typical bull pattern because it is composed of five waves.[30] However, due to its abnormal size, it may be classed as an inverted flat[31] of very large degree because it forms part of a "corrective." Wave ② consumed 5 years.

Triangle wave ③ was down in five waves from 1937 to 1938 and lasted 13 months. Triangle waves ①, ② and ③ therefore constitute a flat, from November 1928 to March 1938.

Triangle wave ④, 1938 to 1939, is an inverted zigzag.

Triangle wave ⑤ from 1939 to April 1942 is a flat.[32] It droops and is very long. Its extreme length was necessary in order to coincide with the overall time period of 13 years from 1928 and 21 years from July 1921.

As stated in Chapter 5, the fifth wave of a triangle may or may not be confined within the outline of a triangle. In this case it exceeded the outline. Nevertheless it is a perfect flat of three waves, marked Ⓐ, Ⓑ, and Ⓒ. Wave Ⓑ is 62% of Wave Ⓐ and 62% of Wave Ⓒ. In other words, waves Ⓐ and Ⓒ are the same length.

---

[30] Absolutely. You will notice that in Figures 72 and 74, Elliott's labels are not consistent with his triangle thesis, but with the correct interpretation. The only exception is that the last wave down should be counted as five waves, completing a zigzag from the 1937 top.

[31] Frost and I discuss this error in our book. It is possible to rationalize any five-wave move as a "three," but only at the expense of the utility of the Wave Principle and what we call the "right look." Flats are so called because they are flat. The B wave of a flat always recedes deep into A-wave territory. In a five-wave move, there is no overlapping of waves, by definition. Therefore the 1932-1937 advance must be classified as a "five."

[32] Again, flats are flat and should not "droop." Actually it is a five-wave decline, with no overlapping, finishing off the zigzag which began in 1937. To count it correctly, put a 1 where Elliott has an a, a 2 where he has a b, a 3 where he has an Ⓐ, a 4 where he has a Ⓑ and a 5 where he has a Ⓒ.

CHAPTER XII

INFLATION

The term "inflation" is defined in the dictionary as "extension beyond natural limits." One bull market does not exceed "natural limits." A series of bull markets, one above the other, would be "beyond natural limits." One bull market would not be "above another" were it not for sub-normal intervening bear markets.

Inflation[33] occurred during the 'Twenties because of sub-normal bear markets. During this period there were three normal bull markets and two sub-normal bear markets, total five.[34] Warnings of inflation occurred in the following order: normal wave 1, sub-normal wave 2, normal wave 3, subnormal wave 4, and penetration of the parallel line by wave 5 on arithmetic scale (see Chapter 9, Figure 65).

Figure 75 pictures a normal bull market and a normal bear correction (waves a, b and c) which penetrates the base line substantially. Figure 76 pictures a sub-normal bear correction that barely penetrates the base line.

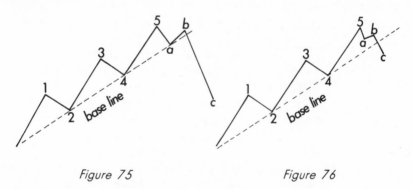

Figure 75   Figure 76

---

[33] Elliott is using a certain dictionary definition of inflation, not the monetary one. By his definition, "inflation" occurs in a market which undergoes acceleration in terms of points advanced per unit of time.
[34] The corrections were certainly sub-normal, and the entire wave was longer than might have been expected. Elliott's reference to and discussion of the three "bull markets" derives from his conclusion that this entire wave was an extension.

Figure 77 shows the Dow-Jones Industrial Average from 1921 to November 1928 on arithmetic scale. Wave 5 penetrates the parallel line. Penetration of the parallel line demands that the entire picture from 1921 should be graphed on log scale. Figure 78 pictures the same average (monthly range) on log scale. Wave 5 touches but does not penetrate the parallel line.

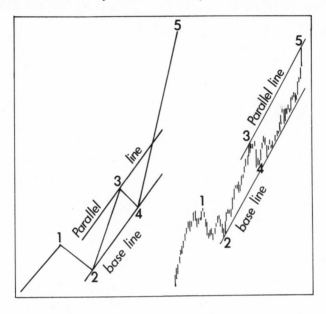

Figure 77   Figure 78

There are three methods of ascertaining in advance at what point, and at what time inflation will terminate: that described above, ratio (described in Figure 71), and time (described in Figure 71).

CHAPTER XIII

PRICE OF GOLD

Another example of the importance of differentiating between the virtues of arithmetic and log scale is the price of gold. The graph of this item covers one bull market from 1250 to 1939, nearly seven centuries. In Figure 79, wave ② is simple and wave ④ is complex. Note the letters Ⓐ, Ⓑ and Ⓒ of wave ④.

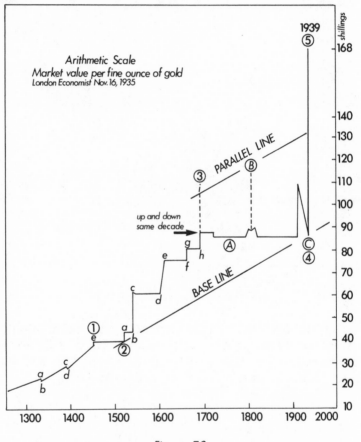

Figure 79

In Figure 79, plotted on arithmetic scale, the price line exceeds the parallel line, therefore semi-log scale is demanded as shown in Figure 80. The parallel line on logarithmic scale indicates the final top of inflation of any human activity.[35] When an advance of five waves is completed <u>within</u> the channel on <u>arithmetic</u> scale, inflation does not exist.

The gradual rise of wave ① in Figure 79 suggests that the market price of gold during that period was "free," that is, not fixed by any authority. Thereafter advances were abrupt and corrections sidewise which indicates that the price was dominated by some authority, presumably political. Corrections may move sidewise, downward, or downward and sidewise as shown in wave ④ of Figure 79.

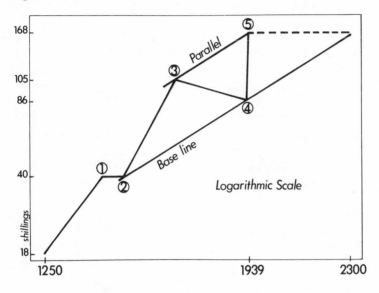

Figure 80

Under the law herein described, when a pattern has been completed, as indicated in Figure 80 on log scale by the contact of wave ⑤ with the parallel line, no further advance in price will occur until <u>after</u> the price line has penetrated the base line at some point. Therefore the probability is that the present price of gold, 168 shillings, will remain stationary, at least until it contacts the base line about the year 2300, as indicated by the junction of the dashed lines at the extreme right of the graph.[36]

---

[35] Elliott did not mention the possibility of extreme currency debasement, which is a human activity. Obviously using the tenets of the Wave Principle to interpret a chart of gold in terms of the hyperinflated German marks of 1923 would be an exercise in futility.
[36] The upper parallel line has since been penetrated, suggesting an extended third wave in development.

CHAPTER XIV

PATENTS

The expression "human activities" includes every activity, not only the stock market, but production, life insurance, movements from cities to farms and vice versa, etc. as shown in miscellaneous items listed in Chapter 3.

Occasionally some rather unusual items present themselves, such as for example patents, which is a human activity but not emotional.[37] Figure 81 is the record of applications for patents from 1850 to 1942. Note the five waves. The fifth wave extended from 1900 to 1929. The Industrial average followed the same pattern during almost the same period (see Figure 82). Note the "correction" of patents from 1929 to 1942 in three waves, A, B and C. Stocks followed the same pattern during the same period, except that from 1928 to 1942 the "correction" was a triangle instead of three waves A, B and C.

In early days, farming was the principal occupation. Here and there a farmer might own a store or manufacture something as a sideline. Manufacturing was on a piece-work basis and performed in the home. Natural resources, climate, genius and democracy in the United States required the formation of corporations to finance individual initiative. Inventions and the introduction of machinery gradually changed everything. The Louisiana Purchase, the conquest of California, the acquisition of Texas and Oregon, together with settlement of boundaries with Mexico and Canada, added immensely valuable territory.

Genius was (and still is) the principal asset. This is demonstrated by the graph of patent applications from 1850 to 1942. Note that the pattern coincides with that of the stock market. The United States is radically different from any other country in one vital aspect -- our

---

[37] The Wave Principle tracks more than the emotional phenomena because it is also a record of the progress of Man, intertwined with his emotions. It can even be postulated that the moods reflected by the averages cause progress; presumably Man will produce more and invent more when the dominant mood is "up" rather than "down."

ancestors hail from all parts of the world. They were dissatisfied with tyranny and politics of their homelands and came here to enjoy liberty and develop their genius.

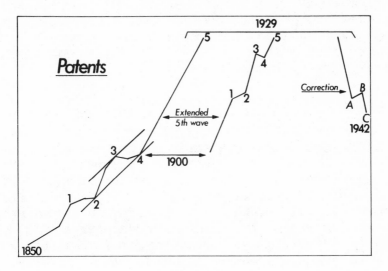

Figure 81

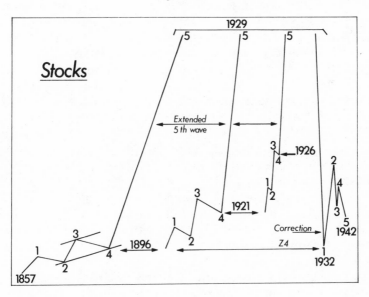

Figure 82

CHAPTER XV

TECHNICAL FEATURES

The movement of one activity is seldom, if ever, a reliable guide for another. Figure 83 shows graphs of three indices -- the London Industrials, the Dow-Jones Industrials and production in the United States. All are plotted from 1928 to January 1943. Production figures are from the Cleveland Trust Company.

The Dow-Jones Industrials (middle graph) registered a five-wave triangle from November 1928 (the orthodox top) to April 1942. The amplitude of each of the second, third and fourth waves of the triangle to its predecessor is approximately 61.8%. The existence of the triangle is proved by its outline, the time element, the composition of each wave, and the uniform ratio of each wave to its predecessor. High speed inflation from 1921 to 1929 (8 years) caused the rapid decline to 1932 (34 months). These, in turn, caused the symmetrical triangle which simulates a pendulum coming to rest.

The triangle disregarded the following events which occurred during its 13-year period: reversal from Republican to New Deal administrations, devaluation of the dollar, repudiation of the gold clause in Government bonds, the shattered two-term precedent, the second World War which started in 1939, and the rise in production, the index of which started upward in 1938 and finished its pattern of five waves in June 1941.

The London Industrials (top graph) did not follow New York stocks in 1929. This index registered tops in January 1929 at 140 and in December 1936 at 143. The lows in 1932 and 1940 were the same, 61. From 1940 to January 1943 this index advanced to 131. Between January 26 and July 28, 1939, the London Industrial average formed a triangle.

London stocks invaded the stratoshpere in 1720, 1815 and 1899 approximately 89 years (FSS) apart. When and if English stocks should inflate it does not follow that ours will do so.

A production index prepared by the Cleveland Trust Co. (bottom graph) registered tops in June 1929 at

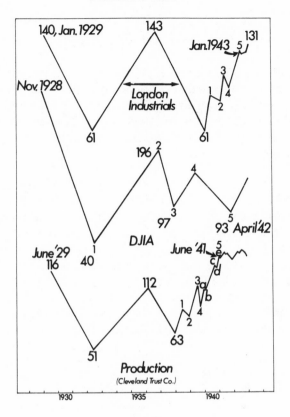

Figure 83

116 and in 1936 at 112, and a low in 1938 at 63. From 63
a complete advance of five waves finished its patterm in
June 1941, before the D-J Industrials started up from the
end of the triangle in April 1942.

During the period from 1857 to 1928 we
participated in three wars, Civil, Spanish and World War
I. Nevertheless the pattern of the Supercycle movement
was perfect, as demonstrated elsewhere.

Stocks and commodities have never inflated in
unison. Therefore, if commodities explore the strato-
sphere it does not follow that stocks will do likewise at
the same time. Commodities inflated in 1864 and 1919 --
55 years apart.[38]

---

[38] And again in 1974. In terms of years, the Fibonacci
number 55 is the length of the so-called Kondratieff Wave.

The worthlessness of news is demonstrated in the next chapter. A financial writer said:

The fact that security prices have been advancing on the good news from Salerno and that they reacted in August on similar good news from Sicily leads students to conclude that the August reaction was due chiefly to technical considerations rather than to military happenings.

One day, London experienced a severe "blitz." London stocks advanced and New York stocks declined. Financial writers in both places stressed the blitz as the cause. At the time, London was in an uptrend and New York in a downtrend. Each followed its pattern regardless of the blitz. The same wave behavior occurred following Mussolini's exit, July 25.

The above analysis proves that technical factors govern the market at all times.

CHAPTER XVI

DOW-JONES RAIL INDEX

An examination of the Rail index is interesting, informative and profitable. Transportation is the most important human factor in our economy because of the great distances between borders since the Louisiana Purchase, the settlement of boundaries with Mexico and Canada, and the additions of Texas and California.

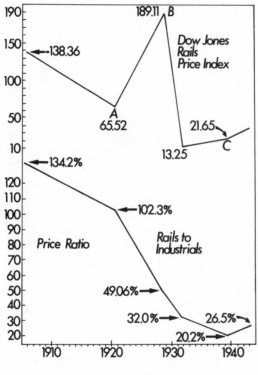

Figure 84

The bottom graph in Figure 84 is the ratio of the Rail index to the Industrial index from 1906 to January 1944. This demonstrates that, in relation to the Industrials, the Rails were persistently weaker from 1906 to 1940 (34 years). The causes of this behavior were excessive proportion of bonds to common stocks, the Panama Canal which opened for business in 1914 (1906 + 8 = 1914), and the automobile and the airplane. These three factors resulted in weakness of both rail bonds and stocks to such an extent that in 1940 one third of rail mileage was in receivership and another third on the borderline.

The second World War temporarily removed Panama Canal competition and otherwise increased rail revenue, both passenger and freight. The extraordinary revenue that the Rails enjoyed since 1940, especially after Pearl Harbor, enabled the railroad companies to reduce their bonded indebtedness and in consequence fixed charges. This benefit is permanent. See Figure 85.

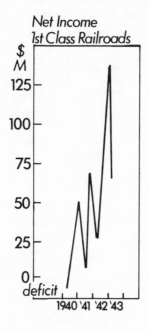

Figure 85

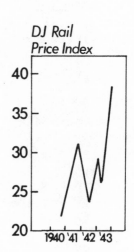

Figure 86

The Rails registered their <u>ratio</u> low point in 1940 and from then to July 1943 advanced as shown in Figure 86. The Industrials bottomed two years later in April 1942 at the end of the thirteen-year triangle.

During the 34 (FSS) year period between 1906 and 1940, the Rails reversed downward before the Industrials and reversed upward after the Industrials. Since 1940 this practice reversed; that is, the Rails have been first to reverse upward and last to reverse downward. This practice may continue for some years.

CHAPTER XVII

THE VALUE OF NEWS

Wall Street has an adage that "news fits the market." This means that, instead of the news "making the market," the market foresees and appraises the importance of the underlying forces that later may become news. At best, news is the tardy recognition of forces that have already been at work for some time and is startling only to those unaware of the trend.

The forces that cause market trends have their origin in nature and human behavior and can be measured in various ways. Forces travel in waves, as demonstrated by Gallileo, Newton and other scientists. These forces can be computed and forecast with considerable accuracy by comparing the structure and extent of the waves.

The futility in relying on anyone's ability to interpret the value of any single news item in terms of the stock market has long been recognized by experienced and successful traders. No single news item or series of developments can be regarded as the underlying cause of any sustained trend. In fact, over a long period of time the same events have had widely different effects, because trend conditions were dissimilar.

This statement can be verified by a casual study of the forty-five year record of the Dow Jones Industrial Average. During that period kings have been assassinated, there have been wars, rumors of wars, booms, panics, bankruptcies, New Era, New Deal, "trust busting," and all sorts of historic and emotional developments. Yet all bull markets acted in the same way, and likewise all bear markets evinced similar characteristics that controlled and measured the response of the market to any type of news as well as the extent and proportions of the component segments of the trend as a whole. These characteristics can be appraised and used to forecast future action of the market, regardless of the news.

There are times when something totally unexpected happens, such as an earthquake. Nevertheless, regardless of the degree of surprise, it seems safe to conclude that any such development is discounted very quickly and <u>without reversing the indicated trend under way before the event.</u>

One of the safeguards in this respect is the willingness of experienced traders to "sell on good news and buy on bad news," especially when such news runs counter to the prevailing trend. This factor tends to upset the expectancy of the public for the market to react directly and in the same manner to similar news at different times.

Those who regard news as the cause of market trends would probably have better luck gambling at race tracks than in relying on their ability to guess correctly the significance of outstanding news items. Mr. X. W. Loeffler of Westwood, New Jersey, publishes a graph of the Dow Jones averages listing the important news events in chronological order (price $1). Examination of this graph shows clearly that the market has advanced and declined on the same kind of news. Therefore the only way to "see the forest clearly" is to take a position above the surrounding trees.

War starts world-wide forces so powerful that they would seemingly dominate all other considerations and drive the market farther and farther in the same direction. At various times war incidents receive front page display. Sharp breaks in the market during August and September, 1937, again in March, August, and September, 1938, and in March-April 1939 all coincided with war developments. Yet when war was actually declared on September 1, 1939, the market advanced violently on tremendous volume. The only satisfactory explanation for this curious behavior is derived from the technical position of the market cycle at these times.

In 1937, 1938 and early 1939, the market had completed important rallies and was resuming the downward trend at the time of the war incidents. Consequently, these "war scares" were construed bearishly and served simply to accelerate the downward trend. On the other hand, the market was in an entirely different postion in September 1939 when the war started. Charts show a downward phase started the latter part of July 1939 as a correction of the upward movement

from mid-April of that year. This downward phase was
fully completed a week before September 1, and in fact
the market advanced briskly during this short period about
ten points from the wave bottom of August.

On the actual announcement of the war, the
market fell sharply during the day to a level fractionally
below the August bottom and then bounded upward with
amazing speed. Those who bought selected stocks at the
bottom in August and on the secondary war-scare bottom
reaped large profits compared with those who tried to buy
stocks in the wild scramble that followed. The late
comers in most cases were sorry they had bought, because
they paid top prices and sold out at substantial losses.
Actually the peak of the market for the steels and other
primary war stocks was reached in less than two weeks
after the start of war. Since then the market has more
consistently placed a bearish construction upon the
outlook for war stocks and war profits because of the
broad bear cycle, which was resumed in the fall of 1939.
In contrast, the effect of World War I (1914-1918) was
primarily bullish due to the type of price cycle from
mid-1913.

When France collapsed early in June 1940, most
people felt that the war would be very short and Hitler
would inevitably overrun England. Waves, however, had
indicated in May, when the Dow Jones Industrial Average
reached 110.61, that the worst of the phase was over and
that stocks should be bought for a substantial
intermediate recovery. Even in the midst of the highly
emotional news from Europe during the first half of June,
the Average reacted only to 110.41.

At the time of the November 1940 election,
sensational news announcements were published regarding
huge expenditures to be made for defense and to aid
England. Most economists and observers reasoned this
would set inflationary forces in motion, and bought
stocks. At the same time, however, waves indicated that
the inflation would not benefit stocks from a price
standpoint and the upward movement since June having
been completed, much lower stock prices would develop.
Subsequently the market declined nearly fifty points.

The general belief that current news affects the market is widespread and even exploited. If current news were responsible for fluctuations, cycles would not occur. Whenever one is inclined to believe in "news," I recommend careful review of the pattern and wave ratios in Figure 71, then recall the events and opinions expressed at numerous times during that twenty-one year period.

CHAPTER XVIII

CHARTING

Students might benefit by detailed suggestions which I have found essential. Model charts are shown in Figure 87.

Accurately observing the lower degrees of waves of a movement requires the daily range of price fluctuations. This high-low range was inaugurated by Dow-Jones in 1928.

The chart spacings recommended for the purpose of emphasizing price fluctuations are a vertical quarter inch for one point of the Industrial Average, a vertical half inch for one point of the Rail Average, and a vertical half inch for one point of the Utility Average. Such spacings on a chart facilitate accurate interpretation. The quarter inch scale is subdivided into fifths, thus eliminating any guesswork as to the exact spot at which to locate the daily range and hourly record.

Likewise it is important to space the distance between days as shown on the model charts. When each verical line of the chart is employed, instead of every other line, the result is that lines of the price range are too cramped for comfortable reading. Do not leave any space for holidays or Sundays.

Precisely the same scale and forms are recommended for the hourly record -- one quarter of an inch horizontally for a session of five hours, or one of the smallest squares for each hour. Do not leave any space following a two hour session on Saturday. Do not show the opening figure. The high-low range for the day should be shown at the end of the last hour of each session. All of these recommendations are portrayed in Figure 87.

Never economize in chart paper at the expense of clarity. When a movement begins on one sheet and terminates on another, clarity is jeapordized. The same is true when a movement is discontinued at the top of the sheet and started again at the bottom.

Chart paper which will properly clarify interpretations of waves is manufactured by Keuffel & Esser and is for sale by them and by large stationery stores. It is available in these sizes: by the yard, 20" wide, in sheets 8 1/2" x 11", and in sheets 10" x 15". Two weights of paper in all three sizes are offered.

It is suggested that charts 10" x 15" be used, and that not more than two averages be charted on one sheet. For example, on one sheet 10" x 15" the daily range of the Industrials and daily volume should be shown, and on another sheet 10" x 15", the daily range of the Rails and Industrials. Use two other sheets 10" x 15", one for the hourly record of the Industrials and the hourly volume of the whole market, and another for the hourly record of the Rails and Utilities, a total of four sheets for the entire program.

For individual stocks and commodities the same general recommendations apply, except that the chart paper should be subdivided by fourths instead of fifths.[39]

The weekly range should be charted on forms of the largest size charts available in order to cover a long period, one for an entire cycle. The monthly range, especially of the averages and groups, is important for observing complete cycles.

Figures 53 and 54 in Chapter 6 demonstrate the value of the daily range in order to establish beforehand the extent and pattern of the weekly range. In like manner the weekly range assists in establishing the extent and pattern of the monthly range. The monthly range assists in establishing the extent of cycles. Likewise the monthly range facilitates observances of monthly time periods and ratio of waves.

In Figure 87 the vertical allowance for the Industrials is one point per quarter inch. The Rails and Utilities are allowed one point per half inch. The weekly range may be reduced to two points per quarter inch for the Industrials and one point per quarter inch for the Rails and Utilities. The monthly range may be reduced still further.

---

[39] For measurements in fractions (eighths and quarters) rather than decimals.

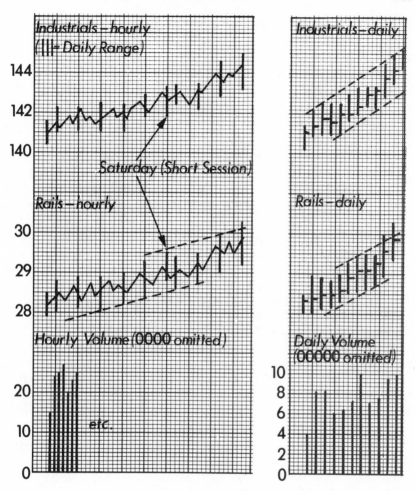

Figure 87

      On the actual chart paper the cross ruled lines
are pale green in color and it will be noted that the chart
patterns, which are drawn in black ink, are accentuated
against the pale green background which is highly
advantageous in reading waves.

CHAPTER XIX

INVESTMENT TIMING

Timing is one of the chief elements in the universe. We separate the times of the year into seasons: spring, summer, fall and winter. We recognize the daylight as the time of activity and the night time for relaxation and rest.

In the matter of investment, timing is the most essential element. What to buy is important, but when to buy is more important. Investment markets themselves progressively foretell their own future. Waves indicate the next movement of the market by their patterns whose beginnings and endings are susceptible to definite and conclusive analysis.

Nature's Law embraces the most important of all elements, timing. Nature's Law is not a system, or method of playing the market, but is a phenomenon which appears to mark the progress of all human activities. Its application to forecasting is revolutionary.

If one had invested $1,000 in long-term Government bonds in January 1932 and sold in June 1939, a total profit of $5000 (including interest and appreciation) would have resulted in the 89-month period. In January 1932, the yield on market value of Governments was 4%. In June 1939 it was only 2%. As for the stock market, an investment of $1,000 in July 1932 would have been increased by March 1937 to approximately $5,000 without taking dividends into account. This statement is based on the per cent change in the popular averages.

The importance of accurate forecasting has resulted in an immense increase in the use of statistics. A comparison of files of newspapers of fifty years ago with those of today will be a revelation in this respect. Millions are being spent to find a satisfactory forecasting device, but the search will be fruitless without recognition of the fact that the habit of the market is to anticipate, not to follow.

CHAPTER XX

SELECTION OF TRADING MEDIA

Chapter 19 demonstrated that the factor of first importance in stock trading is timing, that is, when to buy and sell. The factor of next importance is what stocks to trade. To guide you in selecting securities (either stocks or bonds) in which trading is contemplated, you should keep uppermost in mind all of the following fundamentals.

Fluctuations and Income

Fluctuations in market value of any security are much greater than its income yield, therefore the paramount factor is the preservation and appreciation of principal as a result of price fluctuations.

Bull Market Tops

In bull markets, each group of the 55 Standard Statistics list shows tops made at different times, like a fan. Bull markets are those which develop five primary waves during a period of about two years.[40] During such a period the several groups tend to move rather uniformly, being propelled by the powerful force of the cycle.

Bear Markets

Usually the duration of a bear market is longer than the previous bull market.[41] During the severe and relatively short duration of the decline from 1929 to 1932, the very best stocks and bonds, as well as the lower grades of both, had to be liquidated regardless of their

---

[40] This is an arbitrary definition, and of no value. The definition of a bull market is first and foremost any advance which contains the necessary five waves. The time duration for the definition depends entirely on one's own choice of wave degree for trading or investment.

[41] I think this is an unintentional misstatement. Bear markets are almost always shorter than bull markets, and over the long run tend to run about 61.8% of the time required for bull markets (see Chapter 4 of ELLIOTT WAVE PRINCIPLE -- KEY TO STOCK MARKET PROFITS).

real value. Many traders gained the erroneous impression that the bottoms of all bear markets should repeat that performance.[42] Research indicates many years will elapse before such a drastic decline may be expected.

The final bottoms of bear markets are conspicuous by bottoms of nearly all groups being made simultaneously. This is just the reverse of tops in bull markets. During bear markets, powerful leadership is less pronounced and this is especially true during rallies. During bear swings the market as a whole and the several groups become more sensitive to current events and extraneous factors.

Previous Experience in Trading

Many traders acquire prejudices against certain stocks because of previous unfortunate experiences. To pursue such a course the trader would eventually find no group free from objection.

Inactive Stocks

A stock that is frequently or occasionally inactive should be avoided for trading, the reason being that waves are not registered. Inactivity clearly indicates that the stock does not enjoy thorough distribution, or else it has reached the fully-developed stage.

Inside Tips

Usually inside tips from well-intentioned friends refer to inactive and low priced stocks. It is preferable to confine one's trading to stocks that are always active.

---

[42] The same expectation is prevalent today. With the crashes of 1969-1970 and 1973-1974 behind us, most are currently looking for an "instant replay" at the four-year cycle juncture. Few can envision the possibility of a less "oversold" bottom, despite the fact that the wave position suggests that, as Elliott puts it, "many years will elapse before such a drastic decline may be expected."

The Age of Stocks

The life of a stock usually has three stages. The first is the youthful or experimental stage, during which such stocks should be avoided as they have not been properly seasoned. The second is the creative stage. Stocks that fall within this category have reached healthy development, thus making them a desirable medium for trading, provided they are thoroughly seasoned. The third or grown-up stage represents the period of fullest development. Dividends may be uniformly reliable and fluctuations narrow. For these reasons the certificates become lodged in portfolios and therefore the stock is less attractive for trading purposes.

In summary, when the pattern of a reliable average is favorable, follow these recommendations:

1) Select the groups which perform in harmony with the average.

2) Then select the stocks that move in sympathy with these groups.

3) Always choose stocks that are constantly active, medium priced and seasoned leaders.

4) Diversify funds, i.e., employ more or less an equal number of dollars in from five to ten stocks, not more than one stock of a group (for example: General Motors, United Aircraft, U. S. Rubber, U. S. Steel, New York Central, and Consolidated Edison).

CHAPTER XXI

PYRAMIDIC SYMBOLS
And How They Are Discovered

By permission of the Landone Foundation, I quote three paragraphs from pages 134 and 135 of Mr. Landone's book, Prophecies of Melchi-Zedik.

> The total distance around the base of the Pyramid is 36,524.22 Pyramid inches. This is exactly 100 times 365.2422, the number of days in our solar year.

> The height of the designed Pyramid is 5,813.02 inches.

> These mystic wise men formulated systems of measures of quantity, time, weight and length, and squares and cubes of the lengths. Since all of these are based on the length of the side of the square, and since that length was derived from the circle whose circumference was equal to the days of the solar year, and since the time of revolution of earth around the sun is eternal, these mystics created the only system of measurement forever exact and eternally the same.[43]

Having ascertained the circumference of the Great Pyramid Gizeh at its base, the investigators cast about for some known fact that would correspond. In this instance it was the number of days in a year, down to the last fraction. In other words, two facts are associated and thus establish the purpose of the symbol from which forecasts may be made.

I discovered rhythm in human activities and later learned that it is symbolized in the Great Pyramid. Egyptologists failed to recognize this symbol because they were not aware of rhythm in nature and human activities. This symbolism is described in Chapters 1 and 2, and demonstrated in Chapters 8 through 14.

---

[43] For more on this subject, read Peter Thompkins' Secrets of the Great Pyramid (Harper & Row, 1971).

My contribution to pyramidic symbolism follows, in the order named:

1) Discovery of patterns, degrees and numbers of waves.

2) Association of the Fibonacci number series, Hambidge's discoveries in its application to art and botany, and Pythagoras and his cryptic diagram.

3) Diagrams of the Great Pyramid from all angles.

4) Correlation of the Fibonacci ratio and the elevation of the pyramid -- 5,813 inches (which is composed by the three basic numbers of the Fibonacci Summation Series, 5, 8 and 13) -- to the base of the pyramid.

5) Application of the Summation Series to human activities in many fields.

Ratio Ruler

Draughtsmen use an instrument called a "proportional divider." The fulcrum is movable in order that any ratio may be obtained. These instruments are expensive and now practically unobtainable. I have therefore devised a handy substitute for ascertaining, without mathematical calculations, when the ratio between any two movements, in either amplitude or time, is 61.8%. I will send one on receipt of 25 cents in check, money order, coin or postage stamps.

R. N. Elliott
No. 63 Wall Street
New York (5), N. Y.

CHAPTER XXII

THE LAW OF MOTION

Dictionary definitions of the word "cycle" are several: "a period of time," "an entire turn or circle," "a spiral leaf structure," "a series that repeats itself." Attention has been mainly directed to cyclical rhythms in the stock market where they are very pronounced. Every movement, from wheels to planets, is cyclical. All cycles have subdivisions or degrees which facilitate the measurement of their progress.

Planets travel in orbits and at speeds peculiar to each. The Earth revolves on its own axis and once in every twenty-four hours divides night from day. It encircles the sun once a year and thus provides the four seasons. The mechanism of planetariums may be turned backward or forward to show the relative positions and

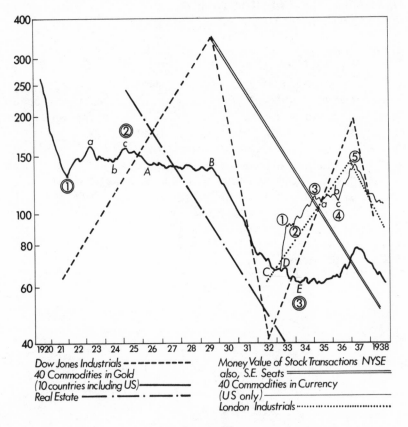

Figure 88

movements of planets and their satellites at any time, past, present or future.

Some elements never change their patterns. For example, water constantly observes complete cycles. The sun's rays on the ocean's surface cause water to evaporate. Air currents move the vapor until it encounters cooler atmosphere over hills and mountains, which in turn condenses the vapor. Gravity draws the water back to earth, where it again joins the sea.

Nations experience political, cultural and economic cycles, both great and small. Patterns of human life are observed in mass movements such as migration to and from cities, average age, birth rate, etc.

Figure 88 demonstrates that one human activity cannot be depended upon to forecast another. Therefore the pattern of each factor must be analyzed by its own waves and not by extraneous factors. During the period from 1939 to April 1942, the lag in the stock market, compared to that of business produced much discussion but no explanation. The answer is that eight years of inflation during the 'Twenties created a thirteen-year triangle to 1942.

The graph of temperature shown in Figure 89 is important. Temperature is not associated with human activities; nevertheless cyclical waves, over a period of one hundred ten years, formed a perfect pattern of five waves upward.

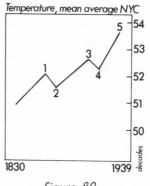

Figure 89

Periodicities between peaks and valleys of many items, such as epidemics, production of lynx pelts, tent caterpillars, salmon runs, etc. are fairly common. In human activities, cycles are not all uniformly spaced. They follow wave patterns in accordance with the Fibonacci Summation Series.

Dynamic symmetry is a law of nature and

therefore the basis of all forms of activity.

Since the discovery that the earth is round, the cycle has been the subject of much research. There are three classes of cycles. First are uniform periodicities between peaks and between nadirs, such as day and night, seasons of the year, tides, epidemics, weather, swarms of insects, etc. (I recommend an article by Donald G. Cooley entitled "Cycles Predict the Future" in Mechanix Illustrated, February, 1944). Second are periodical fluctuations caused, in some instances, by astronomical aspects. Third are patterns, time and ratio, in accordance with a summation series disclosed by the mathematician Fibonacci.

A pamphlet entitled "The Relation of Phyllotaxis to Mechanical Laws" by Professor A. H. Church of Oxford is very interesting. Phyllotaxis is the leaf arrangement of plants. Mr. Jay Hambidge spent many years researching records, and is the author of a book entitled Practical Applications of Dynamic Symmetry. One chapter is entitled "The Law of Phyllotaxis." A copy of pages 27 and 28 thereof is repeated in Chapter 2 of this treatise.

Dr. William F. Petersen, Professor of Pathology at the University of Illinois, is the author of a very important and interesting book entitled The Patient and the Weather. Therein are graphed the progress of disease. The patterns are precisely the same as any other activity, including the stock market.

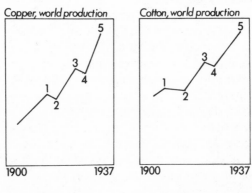

Figure 90   Figure 91

CHAPTER XXIII

THE GREAT DEPRESSION

This common expression is a misnomer insofar as the stock market is concerned. The decline of stocks from 1929 to 1932 was a correction of the previous advance, as shown in Figures 68 and 82. The dictionary defines "depression" as "below the general surface." The Grand Canyon of Colorado is a "depression" because it is far "below the general surface" for many miles on either side. From the top of the Rockies to the Pacific Ocean is a "correction," so to speak, not a "depression," notwithstanding the fact that the Pacific Coast is much lower than the bottom of the Colorado Canyon. There is no such thing as a "depression" in the stock market. If there were, it would be correct to say that from the Rockies to the Pacific is a "depression." There are numerous reasons for this erroneous expression.

The general public, which has no interest in stocks, may have enjoyed and become accustomed to continuous employment in the period from 1921 to 1929. Naturally they assumed it to be a normal condition. When the 1929-1932 decline occurred, many people found it difficult to make both ends meet. Naturally it seemed to them to be a "depression."

During the advance in the stock market from 1921 to 1929, traders in stocks were told that we were in a "New Era," "never would decline," "just keep on going," etc. Many common practices were "awful but lawful."

Many politicians are responsible for the erroneous use of the word "depression." During the early part of the 1929-1932 decline in stocks, when Mr. Hoover was President, some said that prosperity was "just around the corner." During the presidential campaign in 1932 the Democrats blamed the Republicans and Mr. Hoover for the "depression." The results of elections in 1932, 1936 and 1940 demonstrated that most voters believed the New Dealers. The Republicans blamed the New Dealers for the decline from 1937 to 1942. The falsity of this political claptrap, whether sponsored by Democrats or Republicans, is demonstrated graphically in Chapters 10 and 11.

The stock market never has a "depression," it only corrects a previous advance. A cycle is action and reaction.

Many services and financial commentators in newspapers persist in discussing current events as causes of advances and declines. They have available the daily news and market behavior. It is therefore a simple matter to fit one to the other. When news is absent and the market fluctuates they say its behavior is "technical."[44] This feature is discussed in Chapter 17.

Every now and then some important event occurs. If London declines and New York advances, or vice versa, the commentators are befuddled. Mr. Bernard Baruch recently said that prosperity will be with us for several years "regardless of what is done or not done." Think that over.

In the "dark ages," the world was supposed to be flat. We persist in perpetuating similar delusions.

---

[44] Sound familiar? More than thirty years later, this practice is as prevalent as ever.

CHAPTER XXIV

EMOTIONAL CYCLES OF INDIVIDUALS

Cycles of mass psychology in human activities are demonstrated by graphs on other pages. A scientist now discloses his studies in the emotional cycles of individuals. In the November 1945 issue of the Red Book appears an article written by Mr. Myron Stearns in which he reports the results of studies, over a period of seventeen years, made by Dr. Rexford B. Hersey, scientist. The McCall Publishing Corporation has given me permission to quote from the article. I have underlined certain numbers and refer to them in the last paragraph.

Dr. Hersey is a Rhodes scholar, a graduate of the Univesity of West Virginia and the University of Berlin.... Dr. Hersey wrote a book on his findings called "Workers' Emotionalism in Shop and Home," which was published by the University of Pennsylvania in 1932. Far-sighted officials of the Pennsylvania Railroad have supported Hersey's work.... Dr. Hersey was invited to go to Germany. He found that workers there react the same as Americans.

The periodic rise and fall of human emotions are vouched for by Dr. Hersey who has been observing and studying them for more than seventeen years. His researches indicate that with all of us, high spirits and low spirits follow each other with a regularity almost as dependable as the tides. He found that all the checks he made on each man, over a period of weeks, fell into a fairly regular pattern. Dr. Hersey's chart showed that about every 5th week he became more critical.

You take it for granted that a run of bad luck, in time, gets you down unless you exert strong will power. That good news, on the other hand, raises you to the top of the world. Now science says you are wrong. If you are full of energy and enthusiasm, good news will lift you higher still. Or if you are plugging dolefully through Blue Monday, good news may help temporarily, but that is about all.

Human emotions ordinarily rise and fall at regular intervals of from 33 to 36 days. The ups and downs of these factors resemble stock market charts.

The blood cholesterol seems to have a cycle of about 56 days.... The thyroid output, which determines the total emotional cycle, usually makes a round trip from low to high and back in from 4 to 5 weeks.... In hyperthyroid cases, cycles may be as short as 3 weeks.

There seems to be no difference in cycle length between men and women.

The Fibonacci Summation Series includes the numbers 3, 5, 34 and 55. Time cycles are not always exact. Therefore when a period is given as "33 to 36," the basic period is 34, more or less. The basic period of 55 includes "56."

When members of your family, friends, employees, employers, customers, etc. annoy you, I recommend a review of this chapter. Other people have their cycles the same as you do. Do not allow your cycle to tangle with another.

CHAPTER XXV

PYTHAGORAS

Pythagoras, a great man, lived in the fifth century B. C., and made an impression on history that is seldom approached. The reader is urged to review a report on his activities in the Encyclopedia Brittanica. He was a persistent investigator of the discoveries of others and visited Egypt, which is often mentioned as "The Cradle of Civilization."

Pythagoras is prominently known for his studies in mathematics. Insofar as I have seen, the most important of his discoveries has been overlooked. He drew a triangle and placed thereunder the cryptic title "The Secret of the Universe." This feature is described extensively in Chapter 2.

In 1945, Mr. John H. Manas, Ph.D., President of the Pythagorean Society, wrote a book entitled Life's Riddle Solved, in which he disclosed a picture of Pythagoras and I have permission from Mr. Manly P. Hall, head of The Philosophical Society of Los Angeles, California, to repoduce it (see page 232).

There are many symbols in this picture but we will focus our attention on two items, the pyramid which Pythagoras holds in his right hand and the three squares in the lower right hand corner of the picture.

The pyramid represents the Great Pyramid of Gizeh, presumably built about 1,000 B. C., although some students argue that it is much older. This Pyramid is classed as one of the "Seven Wonders of the World." The precision of measurement and placing in position of the immense marble stones employed are remarkable. However, this feature is insignificant when compared to the knowledge symbolized. It may be that a paragraph in the Bible (Isaiah 19:19) refers it. It reads, "In that day shall there be an altar to the Lord in the midst of the land of Egypt, and a pillar at the border thereof to the Lord."

In Chapter 2 are graphed different views of this pyramid. For convenient reference, the view of one side is repeated in Figure 92.

PYTHAGORAS

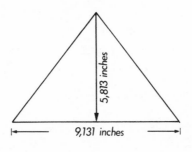

Figure 92

The base of one side is 9,131 inches. The base of the four sides measures 36,524.22 inches. This symbolizes the number of days in our solar year, 365 1/4 days. Our calendar year is 365 days but every fourth year an extra day must be added (February 29th). This is "leap year." The total days in four years is 1,461.

The elevation from base to top is 5,813 inches. The base of one side is 9,131 inches. The ratio of the elevation to the base is 63.6%. The pyramid has five surfaces and eight lines. 5 plus 8 equals 13. Note the elevation, 5,813 inches -- 5, 8 and 13. 5 is 62.5% of 8. 8 is 61.5% of 13. Note the application of this ratio in Figure 71.

In human activities, an advancing movement is composed of five waves, three up and two intervening corrections. A cycle is composed of five waves up and three waves down, total eight. This is true of all degrees, Minor, Intermediate and Major. See Chapter 4.

The diagram shown in the lower right hand of the Pythagoras picture is reproduced as Figure 93. I have numbered the squares which are shaded in the picture. The upper right square has five shaded squares. The upper left square has eight shaded squares. The lower square has thirteen shaded squares. These numbers correspond to the number of inches elevation of the Pyramid.

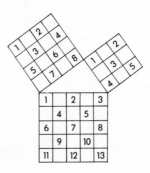

Figure 93

The same three squares are shown in Figure 94. The smaller squares are now numbered in a different manner, that is:

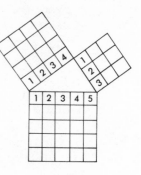

-- 1, 2 and 3, where the square of 3 equals 9,
-- 1, 2, 3, and 4, where the square of 4 equals 16, and
-- 1, 2, 3, 4 and 5, where the square of 5 equals 25.

Figure 94

The theorem is that the square of the hypotenuse of a right triangle is equal to the sum of the squares of the other two sides. The discovery of this solution is the best known of Pythagoras' works.

Now return to the Fibonacci Series, 1 to 144. These numbers form the "Secret of the Universe" to which Pythagoras referred. The best example in botany is the sunflower, described by Mr. Jay Hambidge in Chapter 2. In bodies of humans and animals, the numbers 3 and 5 apply. There are many other symbols in the picture of Pythagoras,[45] which is an idealistic conception.

---

[45] Elliott trimmed the picture to a 5" x 8" Golden Rectangle in his reproduction.

CHAPTER XXVI

MISCELLANEOUS[46]

Volume of Waves

In an advance, the volume of wave 5 does not exceed the volume of wave 3; occasionally it is less. So long as volume increases, another advance is due, until a new high registers without an increase in volume. See Figure 95. Note also that the volume of wave 2 is less than the volume of wave 1. It is a favorable indication.[47]

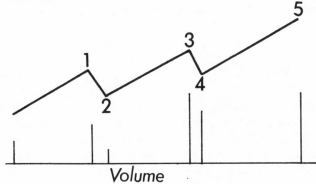

Figure 95

Circles

The word "cycle" means circle. Occasionally this feature appears in graphs of stocks. The circle in Figure 96 is divided into four segments, A, B, C and D. When a graph is rounding downward, as in segment C, and the downward pattern has been completed insofar as the number of waves is concerned, it may be expected that at the bottom, one or more series of "three-wave movements" may develop and then be followed by an accelerated advance as per segment D. The entire

---

[46] This chapter originally contained several paragraphs which fit directly into earlier sections of the book. Apparently Elliott thought of some additional points after the bulk of the manuscript was completed and typed. I have moved these paragraphs to the appropriate areas in the previous text.

[47] That is, indicative that wave 2 is indeed in progress.

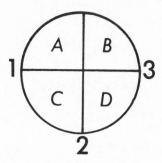

Figure 96

picture down and up will then resemble segments C and D combined, or in other words, the lower half of the circle.

The flood of strikes around the end of 1945 is simply the swing of the pendulum from left to right, 1 to 2 then to 3, as in Figure 96. Before labor was orgainzed (previous to 1906), many, if not most employers, were autocratic, ruthless and heartless to employees, competitors and the public. The behavior of some strikers today is not worse than the behavior of management in early days. Every nation, human activity and individual has its own cycle -- some long, others short, depending on the class and extent of each.

The "A-B Base"

The A-B base[48], shown in Figure 53, Chapter 6, is occasionally composed of double threes or even triple threes, as described in Chapter 5. This is especially true when a rounding bottom is made, as discussed in the first paragraph under "Circles," above.

---

[48] The "A-B base" seems fine as a description for the first two waves of an A-B-C irregular correction. Elliott's reference to Figure 53 seems at first to indicate that that is what he meant. However, in the discussion of the 1942-1946 bull market which follows, he uses the A-B base concept as an additional wave phenomenon which can occur between the end of a corrective wave and the beginning of a cardinal, or impulse wave. Frost and I agree that the addition of this idea is unnecessary, since a construction with that look has been, in our experience, merely part of the previous corrective wave or actually part of the next impulse wave. We have never seen the occurrence of an "A-B base" with no other reasonable explanation.

CHAPTER XXVII

THE 1942-1945 BULL MARKET

The thirteen-year triangle in the Dow-Jones Industrial Average, from 1928 to April 1942 is graphed in Figure 71. As described in Figures 31, 32, 37 and 38 in Chapter 5, thrust follows a triangle.[49]

In Figure 97 the Dow-Jones Industrial Average is graphed. Each vertical line represents the range of one month. Major Wave ① is short. Major wave ③ is longer, and its Intermediate waves are indicated by small letters a, b, c, d and e. Note the inner base line at waves b and d. Major wave ④ is composed of three Intermediate waves indicated by the small letters a, b and c from July to November, 1943. Major wave ⑤ runs from November 1943 to December 10, 1945. Waves A and B consumed five months. In the daily and weekly range for this period, all waves were composed of three waves each (see Figure 53).

From letter B to the number 1 is Intermediate wave 1 as it is composed of five waves of the daily range. Intermediate wave 3 is composed of five waves indicated by small letters a, b, c, d and e (extended). Extensions never appear in more than one of three impulse waves 1, 3 and 5 (see Figures 39 through 44). Intermediate wave 4 is the same as Intermediate wave 2. Intermediate wave 5 is composed of five waves of the weekly range and reached 196.59 on December 10, 1945. The parallel line was slightly exceeded. Subsequent to December 10, 1945, an

---

[49] Elliott's analysis with respect to the action following a triangle would have resulted in a correct conclusion if a triangle had indeed been constructed. However, the triangle concept has led him to expect a sub-normal bear market preceding the next upleg (see Footnote #22).

[50] The "irregular top" of February preceded a clear five-wave decline, as would have been expected. However, this top was probably wave B of an A-B-C irregular correction which constituted wave 4. If Elliott had not used the "A-B base," he might have counted the "A-B" waves as waves 1 and 2 of extended wave ⑤. The December top then would have been marked as the peak of extended wave 3. Wave 4 followed, and then wave 5 to the final orthodox peak at 212.50 in May 1946.

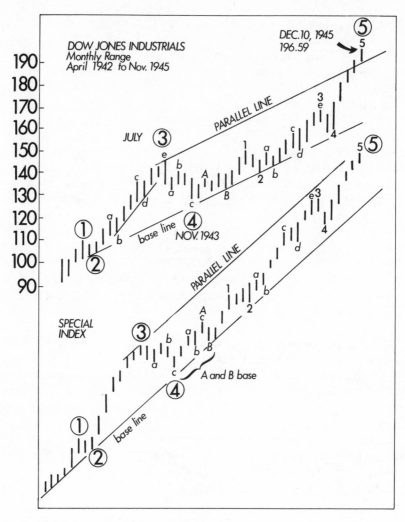

Figure 97

irregular top[50] reached 207.49 on February 4, 1946.

        The pattern of Major wave ⑤ from November 1943 to December 1945 is unusual in one respect. It hugged the base line from November, 1943 to August, 1945, instead of heading straight for the parallel line. The cause of this abnormality was a new crop of reckless speculators with more money than experience who favored low-priced stocks instead of seasoned issues of the type represented by the popular averages. In order to overcome this abnormality, I devised a Special Index that behaved normally, as will be seen in the lower chart of Figure 97. Note that Major wave ⑤ does not hug the base line, but instead follows a straight line from beginning to end.

Note: In the upper graph in Figure 97, the Industrial Average registered its "OT" (orthodox top) at 196.59 on December 10, 1945. On going to press, an irregular top, wave B, is in process of formation. This should be followed by wave C (see Chapter 7).[51]

I expect a sub-normal bear market as illustrated in Figure 76, Chapter 12.

---

[51] Elliott would have been correctly bearish for the 1946 crash, since he was expecting the wave C decline. Since the bottom of the decline was just above 160, he probably would have "called" the bottom as well, since that bottom was at the level of the previous wave 4. The only problem Elliott would have had would have been in expecting the advance to begin again immediately, since he was expecting a sub-normal bear market as a result of the thrust idea, which stemmed from his thirteen-year triangle interpretation. While the lows at 160 were never seriously penetrated, the market did not take off until 1949.

Figure 71 depicted a thirteen-year triangle from 1928 to 1942. By reference to Chapter 5, it will be noted that triangles have always appeared as wave 4 and that wave 5 exceeds the top of wave 3.

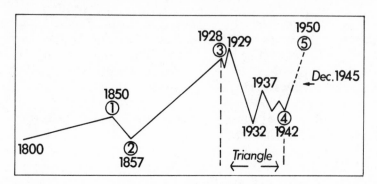

Figure 98

Figure 98 is a graph of the market from 1800 to December 1945.[52] Wave ① from 1800 to 1857 is based on business history, as stock market records are not available previous to 1857. November 1928 is the orthodox top of wave ③ from which the triangle (wave ④) started. The triangle ended and the "thrust" (wave ⑤) started in April 1942. A "thrust" has always exceeded the top of wave ③, which, in this case, is November 1928.

The movement from 1921 to November 1928 was composed of three bull markets and two intervening, sub-normal bear markets. Thus far, in December 1945, one bull market has registered. It would therefore appear

---

[52] Here, with extremely limited data, Elliott outlines correctly the entire Grand Supercycle from the late 1700's. His prediction of a new high above 1929 was also correct, but his short time-frame of 1950 was all out of proportion to the other four waves. It seems that even a cursory examination of the chart would suggest a top much further out than 1950 (and much higher than 328 on the Dow). The problem again is Elliott's 13-year triangle, since thrusts following triangles are generally swift and short. In fact, Elliott first produced this chart in an Interpretive Letter dated August 1941, with two differences. The beginning date was 1776 and the projected ending date was 2012.

logical that the pattern and extent above 1942 would resemble the movement from 1921 to 1928, i.e., three bull markets and two intervening, sub-normal bear markets.

The Dow-Jones Industrial Average started in 1921 at 64 and ended in November 1928 at 299, for a 235-point advance. The thrust started April 1942 at 93. 93 plus 235 equals 328, or 29 points above November 1928, the end of wave ③.[53] The thrust may consume eight years, ending in 1950, similar to 1921-1929. The immense amount of currency in the hands of the public due to financing of the second World War would seem to confirm this indication.

There is a different sequence of procedure now as compared to 1921-1928. During 1921-1928, the first wave was a normal bull market without inflationary symptoms. The fifth wave ending in November 1928 was decidedly inflationary. Now, the first wave, from 1942 to 1945, disclosed inflationary characteristics. Low-priced stocks of questionable value surged ahead at the expense of the "blue chips." The New York Sun selected ninety-six stocks that advanced phenomenally. Every stock started at some figure below $2 per share. The highest rate of advance was 13,300%. The lowest rate of advance was 433%. The average for the group was 2,776%.

---

[53] This computation is based on the tenet that the thrust, or fifth wave following a horizontal triangle, is generally about as long as the widest part of the triangle.

The patterns of graphs shown on previous pages furnish an historic outline of the United States. Its development is marvelous for many reasons:

-- Geographic position, shape and boundaries: A square, bounded on two sides by large oceans, and on two sides by friendly neighbors.

-- Latitude and climate: Semi-tropical, thus facilitating agriculture.

-- Natural resources: Gold, iron, coal, oil, timber and waterways.

-- Genius and individual initiative: The number and value of patents from 1850 to 1929 is marvelous. Attention is invited to Chapter 14. Note that the graph of patent applications (Figure 81) coincides with waves of the stock market, both in time and pattern, which in turn reflects business activity and mass psychology.

-- Democratic ideals: The form of government stimulates individual initiative. This does not imply that perfection has been achieved, but it does suggest that we may be on the right road.

REFERENCES

-- Pythagoras (Greek philosopher, 500 B. C.). See Encyclopedia Brittanica.

-- Fibonacci (Italian mathematician of the thirteenth century. Better known as Leonardo of Piza). His works were published by Count N. Boncampagni, 1857-1862.

-- Dynamic Symmetry ("The Greek Vase"), by Jay Hambidge. Note appendix, pages 146-159.

-- Practical Applications of Dynamic Symmetry ("The Law of Phyllotaxis"), by Jay Hambidge. See pages 27-29.

-- Nature's Harmonic Unity, by Samuel Coleman and C. Arthur Coan.

-- Proportional Form, by Samuel Coleman and C. Arthur Coan. See pages 34-35, 149-155.

-- Curves of Light, by Thomas A. Cook.

-- The Human Situation, by William Macniele Dixon. See pages 129-131.

-- Prophecies of Melchi-Zedik in The Great Pyramid, by Brown Landone.

-- Nuggets from King Solomon's Mine, by John Barnes Schmalz.

OUR FINANCIAL NEWSLETTERS

THE ELLIOTT WAVE THEORIST has earned its reputation as one of the most highly respected financial newsletters in the world. Each 10-page monthly issue thoroughly analyzes Elliott waves, Fibonacci relationships, fixed time cycles, momentum, sentiment and supply-demand factors in a comprehensive approach covering STOCKS, PRECIOUS METALS, INTEREST RATES and the ECONOMY. Forecasts continually zero in on the most likely future path of the markets, and are based on all sizes of trend, from hourly waves to waves lasting over a century.

How well do we perform for you? Don't take *our* word for it. (In fact, you should never buy a service if their *own* assessment of its receord is the only one available!) Just read the quotations below, a sampling of what the *independent* performance rating services have had to say about the accurate market timing record of THE ELLIOTT WAVE THEORIST:

ROBERT PRECHTER

THE ELLIOTT WAVE THEORIST

June 4, 1984

DJIA WAVE STATUS: SUMMARY and OUTLOOK

WAVE DEGREE	DATE BEGAN	WAVE NUMBER	CURRENT DIRECTION	SIGNIFICANCE TO	OPTIMUM STRATEGY	TARGET	ALTERNATE COUNT
GRAND SUPERCYCLE	1789	---	UP, PEAKING	U.S. SURVIVAL	NO ACTION WARRANTED	3684	---
SUPERCYCLE	JULY 8, 1932	(V)	UP	ECONOMIC CONDITIONS	ECONOMY PEAKING	3684	---
CYCLE	AUG 12, 1982	V	UP	INSTITUTIONAL INVESTOR	HOLD LONG	3684	---
PRIMARY	MAY 30, 1984	③	UP	INSTITUTIONAL TRADER	BUY	2000	⑦
INTERMEDIATE	MAY 30, 1:00	(1)	UP	INDIVIDUAL INVESTOR	BUY	1290-1340	(5)
MINOR	MAY 30, 1:00	1	UP	INDIVIDUAL TRADER	BUY	1180	A
MINUTE	MAY 30, 1:00	1	UP	OPTION/FUTURE TRADER	BUY	1155	---
MINUETTE	MAY 31, 1:00	1	UP, PEAKING	SCALPER	SELL	1125	---
SUBMINUETTE	JUNE 1, 3:00	5	UP, PEAKING	SKIMMER	SELL	----	---

THE BOTTOM LINE
The stock market hit the minimum downside target of "1090 in the fourth week of May" on the May 30 reading of Dow 1087.93. Selloffs of any type should now be used for aggressive buying. Next support is Dow 1055, but with all trading cycles in the time zone for a bottom, that level now seems unlikely as a target. The Dow should climb to 1290-1340 by year-end. The bond market ended a one-year decline on May 30, hitting the long-standing Elliott target of "59 3/4-60 1/4" basis the nearby December contract with a dramatic reversal off a spike low at 59 1/2 on the June contract. The upside target by late this year is 73, which should bring long term interest rates back from 14% to near 11%. Targets of "below $300" for gold and "below $6" for silver remain intact, but a move in bullion above $407 basis London fix would force a change in my intermediate term opinion to bullish.

ITEMS OF NOTE
The final results in the United States Trading Championship will be published in a few days. Sincere thanks to all of you for your support and encouragement. Whether or not my monitored account in the options division comes in first, it has produced a return commensurate with the high standards possible under Elliott Wave analysis.

The Futures seminar in Los Angeles June 22-23 described in the enclosed flyer will include my two-hour "mini-seminar" on the Wave Principle. For more info, call 1-800-257-4142.

★ *"A record of uncanny accuracy"*—Investor's Digest ★ *"Single best record"*—Gold Newsletter ★ *"Consistently one of the top-rated chartists in the U.S."*—Western Mining News ★ *"Unequalled by any other forecaster"*—Investor's Digest ★ *"Top rating among the 16 newsletters for accuracy"*—Futures Magazine ★ *"Best short term timer"*—Technical Digest ★ *"Newsletter award for excellence — 1984 and 1987"* — Hard Money Digest ★ *"Best market predictor"*—Investor's Notebook ★ *"Best of the best"* for intermediate term timing in Stocks, Bonds, & Gold—Rating the Stock Selectors ★ *"EWT called for explosive up move right on target."*—Mannie Webb, R.S.S. ★ *EWT has had 6 profitable years in a row in the stock market, each in double digits*—Hulbert Financial Digest ★ *One of the top 10 personal finance newsletters in the world out of more than 100 screened. "Must reading."*—Hayes Investigative Report ★ *EWT is the only service in the country to show a profit in each of the last five years for all futures trading recommendations after $100 per trade is deducted for commissions and "slippage."*—Commodity Traders Consumers Report ★ *"If we had an award for best timer over the past 5 years, EWT's index would be best."*—Timer Digest ★ *"Robert Prechter had every market nailed, and those who followed his Elliott Wave Theorist last year must have been among the most satisfied newsletter subscribers around."*—Wealth Magazine ★ *"For specific, clear market advice, the EWT is superb."*—Investment Highlights.

THE ELLIOTT WAVE THEORIST's accuracy in market timing is a matter of public record, but its value is evident in other ways as well. Many issues contain special features: a detailed analysis of the silver market, for instance, or a discussion of the Grand Supercycle from the 1700s. Special Reports, issued irregularly, have taken an in-depth look at commodity prices, historical parallels, cycle theory, Fibonacci ratio application, and long term forecasts for the economy and the markets. In between regular issues, Mr. Prechter will issue a quick one-page special alert whenever important market changes occur. All this combines to produce the most fascinating and useful investment publication in the world.

HE CAPITAL PRESERVATION STRATEGIST

Throughout the 1970s and 1980s, forecasting the markets and providing rategies for profit were the most important financial functions that a market ser- ce could provide. That is no longer the case. To survive the decade of the 1990s ll require airtight strategies for capital preservation and perhaps even for per- onal survival.

THE CAPITAL PRESERVATION STRATEGIST, edited by international finan- al survival expert Jean-Pierre Louvet, addresses all the important factors cessary to benefit from the monumental implications of the Grand Supercycle p in social mood. CPS answers critical questions regarding bank safety, gold rchases, insurance strategies, estate planning, T-bill ownership, currency note orage and transferring and storing survival capital in foreign countries.

If you wish to protect your finances, yourself and your family against even the ssibility of difficult times in the 1990s, Mr. Louvet's commentary is essential ading.

Mr. Louvet is also author of THE COMING INVESTMENT WAR -- HOW TO WIN (see products beginning on next page).

HE ELLIOTT WAVE Currency & Commodity Forecast

designed for speculators and hedgers who wish to recognize tradable turning ints in the physical commodities and currencies. EWCF sifts through charts of er 25 commodities, currencies and indexes using the Wave Principle, Fibonac- calculations and supporting technical methods, to identify the key emerging arkets with the best profit potential for you each and every month.

Domestic and worldwide events are oducing changes which could amatically affect the way the world does nd pays for) business. This analysis of e markets and the economy will give u an opportunity to take advantage of e profit opportunities which arise in the rrency and commodity markets.

The ELLIOTT WAVE CURRENCY & MMODITY FORECAST is published conjunction with Robert Prechter's wsletter, THE ELLIOTT WAVE EORIST. Together, the two newslet- s monitor every significant market. nce THE ELLIOTT WAVE THEORIST d THE ELLIOTT WAVE CURRENCY & MMODITY FORECAST complement ch other so well, we hope you will make th publications a part of your invest- nt input.

EWCF is edited by two market analysts o specialize in Elliott Wave, cyclic and hnical analysis. One covers curren- s, the other commodities.

The Elliott Wave CURRENCY & COMMODITY FORECAST

$249 per year

THE ELLIOTT WAVE THEORIST

WAVE STATUS OF KEY COMMODITIES

COMMODITY	INTERMEDIATE DEGREE				MINOR DEGREE			
	WAVE NUMBER	CURRENT DIRECTION	TARGET	ALTERNATE COUNT	WAVE NUMBER	CURRENT DIRECTION	TARGET	ALTERNATE COUNT
CRB	(1)	DOWN	237 00 238 00	(r)	3	DOWN	237 00 238 00	5
SWISS FRANC	(4)	UP	66 50 67 50	(5)	a	UP	-	1
MARK	(4)	UP	55 00 55 75	(5)	a	UP		1
YEN	(3)	DOWN	67 00 69 00	(5)	2	UP	77 00 78 50	1
PLATINUM	(3)	DOWN	BELOW 350 00	(c)	3	DOWN	490 00 500 00	-
COPPER	(e)	UP	102 00 107 00	(3)	a	UP		3
CRUDE OIL	(b)	DOWN	15 00 15 50	(1)	r	DOWN	15 00 15 50	3
SUGAR	(1)	DOWN	9 75 10 00	(x)	5	DOWN	9 75 10 00	c

THE BOTTOM LINE
The CRB index has renewed its long term downtrend after completing wave X. Wave (3) in the U.S. DOLLAR has rested on target and its wave (4) correction has begun. The GRAINS have retraced 50% of their initial decline and have resumed their downward trend that began in June. The LIVESTOCK sector should continue firm short term and then decline into the fall. The uptrend in SUGAR that ended in July has resulted in a five wave decline that is expected to find support just under 10 cents.

ITEMS OF NOTE
Our last scheduled ELLIOTT WAVE INTENSIVE WEEKEND WORKSHOP September 10 and 11 in Atlanta is filling up fast. You will learn real time trading strategy. Call 404-536-0309 for information. Please read the enclosed postcard. Have NLI send a free issue of EWCF to your friends, and extend your sub- scription two free months for each new full year subscriber registered through your recommendation.

In June I mentioned that Investment Hotline Monitor would soon release this year's track record for EWCF's Short Term Traders Commodity Hotline. The results are now in and show that EWCF has returned 259% on average required margin for the first six months of 1988 (EWCF's first rating period). With the newsletter producing a profit of 128% on minimum margin (according to CTCR) and the telephone hotline returning 259% profit, 1988 has been good to us. Here's to continued profits!

SPECIAL REPORT COLLECTION, 1981 to date, by Robert R. Prechter, Jr. A timeless compilation of 16 classic essays, including Cyclic Analysis in the Financial Markets; End of an Era; The Advance-Decline Line; Fibonacci in the Stock Market; The Superbull Market of the '80's; Popular Culture and the Stock Market; A Rising Tide; and What A Trader Really Needs To Be Successful; 122 8½"x11" pages.

ELLIOTT WAVE THEORIST REPRINTS, 1976 to date, by Robert R. Prechter, Jr. All published issues including special reports. (Early years published irregularly.) Perfect for earning how to apply "Elliott" in real time! 1983 through 1987 particularly recommended.

ELLIOTT WAVE CURRENCY & COMMODITY FORECAST REPRINTS, July 1983 to date. All issues including special reports.

FIBONACCI NUMBERS, by N. Vorobev. A thorough analysis of the mathematical properties of the Fibonacci number sequence. Moves from "beginner" level to advanced equations. Includes the Golden Section, Golden Rectangle, pentagonal star, Pascal's triangle, continued fractions, Binet's formula, binomial coefficients, some trigonometry and elementary calculus! Hardback.

LEONARD OF PISA AND THE NEW MATHEMATICS OF THE MIDDLE AGES, by Joseph and Frances Gies. A wonderful book about Leonardo Fibonacci's rediscovery of the Golden Ratio in the 13th century. Includes the Golden Rectangle, Fibonacci's own math problems (with solutions!), quaint illustrations. 128 p., hardback.

A TURN IN THE TIDAL WAVE,
by Robert R. Prechter. This major document is the result of years of data compilation and research. It presents a fascinating long term outlook and analysis for the United States stock market, the economy, the U.S. dollar, gold, silver, inflation/deflation, bonds, real estate, collectibles, debt, politics, popular culture and finally, a dramatized scenario for the 1990s that is certain to kick your imagination into gear. If Mr. Prechter's outlook is realized, it will dwarf the importance of both the 1980s' bull market and the 1987 crash. A TURN IN THE TIDAL WAVE presents a powerful case that demands the attention of every serious and prudent market observer. A TURN IN THE TIDAL WAVE contains 110 pages and 40 charts.

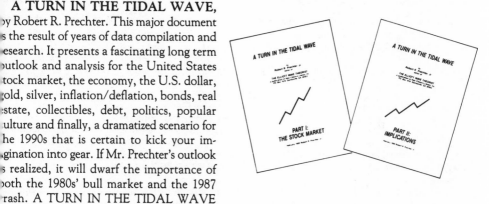

THE COMING INVESTMENT WAR - HOW TO WIN IT, by Jean-Pierre Louvet. Published in January 1990, well **before** the global recession started! This intriguing work is the result of Mr. Louvet's professional lifetime of experience in the field of global financial consulting and asset allocation. It offers a unique geo-political perspective and details a "How To" approach for dealing with the expected risks we will all face this decade.

A PHILOSOPHY OF MARKETS (plus) THE OUTLOOK FOR STOCKS, GOLD AND THE ECONOMY, by A. J. Frost. The first monograph in nearly 20 years from the legendary "dean of Elliott Wave analysis." A.J.'s philosophy of markets, universal law and the human experience, plus an outlook for the markets from September 1989. 30 pages.

PRECISION RATIO COMPASS

Makes Fibonacci and Gann Analysis Easy. Now you can use a truly professional forecasting tool to help *you* forecast turning points in the major financial markets. With the Precision Ratio Compass you'll save time, obtain greater accuracy, and project *price and time* targets with ease. You can quickly and efficiently mark your charts with retracements, multiples, third and fourth generation Fibonacci ratios, and *all other ratios as well.* Even Gann's "squaring of price and time" targets are a snap! You don't have to calculate the distances, write down the figures, and then laboriously transfer the results to your charts. You won't even have to check your records to see what the turning point values are! Your compass knows that when you place it on the chart.

With Complete Instruction Manual. An in-depth, 70-page manual is included with the Precision Ratio Compass to teach you, clearly and simply, how to project price and time targets in the markets. The reference manual includes *never-before published uses of the Fibonacci ratio,* developed by Robert Prechter of THE ELLIOTT WAVE THEORIST after ten years of research. 45 detailed diagrams illustrate the exercises and practical applications.

CONTENTS

- What Fibonacci Ratios Are
- Why Fibonacci Ratios Occur in Markets
- A Complete List of Known Reliable Relationships within Elliott Wave
  Patterns   Impulse Waves   Corrective Waves
- Compass Terminology
- Compass Scales
- What the Compass Does
- Chart Scales
- Price and Time
- Instant Calculations
    Contracting Ratios; Retracements
    Expanding Ratios; Multiples
- Advanced Ratio Application—A Comprehensive Forecasting Method
- The Gann-Blitz Approach
- Gann Range Subdivisions
- Gann Analysis—The Squaring of Price and Time
    1 X 1 lines   2 X 1 lines   1 X 2 lines
- Real-Time Examples of Fibonacci Multiples and Retracements

Incredible Low Price. Other technical "measuring" tools, often made of breakable plastic or cheap aluminum, have sold for as much as $500! Now look at the value you get. Only $249 gives you much more than you'd ever expect in this world of commodity product "overcharge." To start with, draftsmen's tools of this quality sell for up to $120 each in stores, if you want to waste the time and gas to find them. And only the PRC was specifically designed with the Golden Ratio precisely marked on the scale. The quality metal case is built specially for this tool, and is an "extra" we're happy to include. But most important, the PRC Utility Manual explains Fibonacci Ratio application, Gann's Squaring of Price and Time, and includes never-before-published descriptions of where to expect Fibonacci relationships in the price structure of markets. "Secrets" like these have sold for up to *$5000* in commodity courses, and many of these are just plain unavailable *anywhere else.* It's a sound investment in *your* market timing ability. Whether your interest lies in stocks, bonds, precious metals, or commodities, the Precision Ratio Compass can help you make more money in the marketplace.

Money Back Guarantee. Your satisfaction is absolutely guaranteed. Order your Precision Ratio Compass. When you receive it, examine it with care. Test it out on your charts. If you're not completely satisfied in every respect, simply return it within 30 days. We'll promptly refund your purchase price — no questions asked.

New! INSTRUCTIONAL VIDEOTAPE.

As a SPECIAL BONUS, you will receive a PRC INSTRUCTIONAL VIDEO at NO ADDITIONAL CHARGE. This 45-minute instructional video tape features a live workshop presentation by David A. Allman, Director of Research with The Elliott Wave Theorist, demonstrating the use of your Precision Ratio Compass. Learn to mark all Fibonacci ratio retracements and projections on your charts in seconds while enjoying the experience of joining 180 market students at our legendary 1988 Elliott Wave Intensive Weekend Workshop.

You Get Quality For Your Money.

R. N. Elliott used a time-saving Fibonacci ratio ruler, and his mention of it in "Nature's Law" prompted many requests for a similar tool. We took our time and produced a real quality product. See for yourself:

- ✔ Price and time targets can be projected and marked *right on the chart.*
- ✔ Calculates not only *all* Fibonacci ratios, but *ALL RATIOS OF ANY TYPE!*
- ✔ Made of chromium plated solid brass.
- ✔ Lock nut can be quickly hand-tightened to firmly lock the spread between points.
- ✔ The compass points are sharp and true.
- ✔ The durable metal case keeps your fine tool protected at all times.

THE ELLIOTT WAVE EDUCATIONAL VIDEO SERIES, by Robert Prechter is the most professional video product ever to come out of Wall Street. The complete series of 10 tapes provides professional instruction on Elliott Wave analysis. More than 1500 man hours went into preparation to bring you this high quality series. These tapes have been edited for beautiful clarity. The series goes from basic to advanced instruction of the Elliott Wave Principle and can be viewed time and time again. You also receive a set of workbooks containing all of the charts and graphics used during the actual presentation. Also included is our Precision Ratio Compass and manual. If one word could summarize these tapes, that word would be VALUE.

1. INTRODUCTION TO THE ELLIOTT WAVE PRINCIPLE—Robert R. Prechter, Jr. An historical perspective and foundation upon which all essential Elliott Wave education is built. Mr. Prechter shows you step-by-step how the psychological forces within the markets construct the basic Elliott patterns and how those patterns can be easily recognized. You'll learn:
—*The three unbreakable rules of Elliott* —*How to identify the basic five wave pattern* —*How to recognize corrective waves* —*How to apply the key guidelines of equality and alternation* —*The difference between the wave personalities of stocks and commodities* —*The long term wave structure in stocks from the 1700s, the long term wave structure in gold.*

2. COUNTING WAVES CORRECTLY—Robert R. Prechter, Jr.
—*How to apply the Wave Principle to **every** market, from stocks to cocoa* —*How to apply the three rules of Elliott that will separate you from 90% of the self appointed "professionals" using Elliott today* —*How to avoid common pitfalls that lead to incorrect counting* —*How to count waves as they subdivide into smaller degrees* —*How to recognize triangles and apply them to forecasting* —*Finally, you will test your knowledge with the Wave Counting Quiz.*

3. CHARACTERISTICS OF IMPULSE WAVES—David A. Allman
—*How to identify five wave structures at all levels of degree* —*How to identify both types of diagonal triangles and where they are most likely to occur* —*When to expect extensions and how to count them* —*When failures are most likely to occur and how to avoid being caught by surprise when they do occur* —*The correct subdivisions of each of the impulse patterns.*

4. CHARACTERISTICS OF CORRECTIVE WAVES—David A. Allman
—*How to easily identify the two major families of corrections* —*How to correctly label and count corrective patterns* —*How each corrective pattern subdivides* —*Which patterns tell you to expect new highs within the correction* — *When to expect explosive price action after a correction*

5. RULES, GUIDELINES AND WAVE PERSONALITIES—David A. Allman
—*How to apply the rules and guidelines of the Wave Principle to every pattern at the same time to generate the highest probability wave count* —*How the "personalities" of each type of wave can make pattern recognition crystal clear*

6. UNDERSTANDING THE FIBONACCI RATIO IN FINANCIAL MARKETS—Robert R. Prechter, Jr.
—*The logic behind Fibonacci Ratios* —*How the Fibonacci sequence is constructed* —*How Elliott's description of the market's behavior anticipated Mandelbrot's modern concept of Fracial Geometry in natural structures* —*How the Fibonacci ratio is the governor of growth and decay in nature as well as progress and regress in the market place* —*How the small trends in the market become the building blocks for larger trends* —*How Fibonacci is applied to market analysis under the Wave Principle* —*The most common and useful Fibonacci relationships within patterns in markets and how to anticipate their occurrance.*

7. CALCULATING FIBONACCI RELATIONSHIPS WITH THE PRECISION RATIO COMPASS—David A. Allman
—*Detailed, step-by-step instructions on how to use the Precision Ratio Compass as a time saving device when calculating Fibonacci ratios and marking Elliott Wave targets on charts.*

8. REAL TIME TRADING USING THE ELLIOTT WAVE PRINCIPLE—Daniel L. Ascani
—*How to use the Wave Principle to forecast major turning points* —*How to apply the Wave Principle at each step of a developing market trend* —*How to apply probabilities in order to develop preferred and alternate wave counts* —*How Elliott can signal you when risk is low* —*How to know when **not** to enter a trade* —*How to place a stop loss at the most logical point during a trade.*

9. TRADING OPTIONS SUCCESSFULLY USING THE ELLIOTT WAVE PRINCIPLE—Robert R. Prechter, Jr.
—*How five variables govern prices in the options market* —*How to use one tactic to master most of the variables at once* —*Robert Prechter's three "MUSTS" for successful options trading* —*How to apply the money management principles that Mr. Prechter used in setting the all time profit record in the US Trading Championship.*

10. QUESTIONS AND ANSWERS / PRECHTER, ALLMAN & ASCANI
—*A compilation of the most interesting questions and informative answers to a wide variety of topics, including the Elliott Wave Principle, Fibonacci ratios, supporting technical indicators, calculating the dollar weighted put/call ratio, and the time weighted futures premium indicator, and much more.*

NEW CLASSICS LIBRARY, INC.
P.O. BOX 1618 GAINESVILLE, GA 30503

Please send the items listed. Payment, including postage, is enclosed. (Important: please pay only in US$). For more info or immediate shipment, call (404) 536-0309 with VISA or MC#. For TOLL FREE service inside U.S. call 1-800-336-1618.

NAME _____
<small>(In USA, street address for shipping UPS is best)</small>

ADDRESS _____

_____

PHONE _____

Check enclosed ☐ or charge my ☐ VISA ☐ MC

#_____Exp. date_____

☐ The Elliott Wave Theorist (1 year)	$ 233.00 *
☐ The Capital Preservation Strategist	$ 139.00 *
☐ The Elliott Wave Currency & Commodity Forecast	$ 249.00 *
☐ Elliott Wave Principle	$ 21.00
☐ Major Works	$ 34.00
☐ Special Report Collection	$ 39.00
☐ Elliott Wave Theorist Reprints (per calendar yr.)	$ 34.00
☐ Currency & Commodity Forecast Reprints (per yr.)	$ 34.00
☐ Fibonacci Numbers	$ 12.00
☐ Leonard of Pisa	$ 13.00
☐ A Turn In The Tidal Wave	$ 75.00
☐ 1989 & Beyond	$ 20.00
☐ A Philosophy Of Markets	$ 29.00
☐ Precision Ratio Compass with Manual & Video	$ 249.00
☐ Elliott Wave Educational Video Series	$ 1499.00 * *

Indicate Format ☐ VHS ☐ PAL ☐ BETA

POSTAGE & HANDLING (check one):

☐ U.S. and CANADA: <u>add $3</u> 1st item, $2 ea. addt'l item

☐ EUROPE AIRMAIL: <u>add $7</u> 1st item, $4 ea. addt'l item

☐ ALL OTHER CONTINENTS: <u>add $12</u> 1st item, $5 ea. addt'l item

TOTAL $		
GA residents add SALES TAX:		
TOTAL POSTAGE:		
TOTAL ENCLOSED:		

Note: U.S. items are shipped UPS when possible; USPS to P.O. boxes.
Availability and prices subject to change without notice.
Georgia residents add appropriate sales tax.

* Overseas add $17.
* * Overseas add $50.

SPECIAL COUPON
Return this coupon with your order and take **$10** off **any** purchase or **$30** off **any purchase over $250.**
Send VISA or MasterCard information or your check to:
NEW CLASSICS LIBRARY, INC.
P.O. Box 1618
Gainesville, Georgia USA 30503
For more information, telephone 1-800-336-1618
(inside U.S.), or 1-404-536-0309.